TAKING IT PERSONALLY

HOW YOUR CATHOLIC FAITH CAN

transform you

TAKING IT PERSONALLY

HOW YOUR CATHOLIC FAITH CAN
transform you

LEO ZANCHETTIN

The Word Among Us
9639 Doctor Perry Road
Ijamsville, Maryland 21754
www.wordamongus.org

ISBN: 1-59325-062-2

10 09 08 07 06   1 2 3 4 5

Cover Design: Laura Steur-Alvarez
Book Design: Evelyn Harris

Made and printed in the United States of America.

Library of Congress Cataloging-in-Publication Data

Taking it personally : how your Catholic faith can transform you / edited by Leo Zanchettin.
   p. cm.
   ISBN 1-59325-062-2 (alk. paper)
1. Christian life--Catholic authors. 2. Christian life--Biblical teaching. I. Zanchettin, Leo.
   BX2350.3.T35 2006
   248.4'82--dc22
                         2005035351

ACKNOWLEDGMENTS

The chapters in this book are adaptations of articles that first appeared in *The Word Among Us* magazine, for which I have had the pleasure of writing for more than twenty years and editing for ten years. Much of what appears here owes its origins to the magazine's publisher, Joe Difato, and to his mother, Edie, without whose tireless devotion the magazine—and hence, this book—would not exist. I owe a debt of gratitude to Joe and Edie that words cannot express, both for the witness of their lives and for their spiritual guidance and teaching. In addition, I would like to thank Jeff Smith, president of The Word Among Us, Inc., whose friendship and brotherhood I have valued for many long years.

Thanks go also to Patricia Mitchell, my colleague at The Word Among Us Press, whose professional input and friendship I value greatly. Her patience and flexibility have given me the freedom to work on this project in a way that has preserved my sanity. Thanks, too, go to Evelyn Bence, who collated and organized the original material. And finally, to my wife, Katie, who has endured my absence at various points in the production of this book, I owe my heart and my joy.

And even though it goes without saying, I will say it anyway: I want to thank Jesus Christ for bringing me out of darkness and into the light of his love so that I could indeed take it personally.

Leo Zanchettin

CONTENTS

INTRODUCTION

I'll never forget the first time someone tried to evangelize me. I was a college student, and this fellow lived in the same dorm building that I did. "Are you a Christian?" he asked on the day we all moved in for a new school year.

I really didn't know what to make of the question. "Well," I responded. "I'm a Catholic. Does that count?"

"But do you have a relationship with Jesus Christ?" he persisted.

"Well, I go to Mass and say my prayers every morning and night. And there was that time a couple of years ago when I really felt like God was with me."

"But do you know Jesus as your personal Lord and Savior?"

And so the conversation went, with both of us growing increasingly frustrated. We were both traditional Catholics, raised on parochial school, weekly Mass, and once-a-month confessions, but he had a very different approach to Catholicism than I had.

For some reason, this fellow kept pursuing me all semester long, trying to convince me to join his Bible study or to read different books about how to know Jesus as my personal Savior. I guess he liked a good challenge! I was always respectful toward him but remained aloof. I had been so immersed in the formal, liturgical, and institutional life of the church that I didn't know how to respond when he spoke about things on a personal level. I equated his emphasis on an individual conversion experience with "old-time Protestant" religion and tried to convince myself that there was no room for this kind of spirituality in Catholicism. And I was completely wrong.

Why Not?

Through a series of circumstances—some positive and some more difficult—I came to realize that there was something very important in what this fellow was saying. If God was my Father in heaven, why shouldn't I want to get to know him in a personal way? If Jesus really did come to earth as a man, and if he really did ascend to heaven as a man, why couldn't I talk to him and hear him talking to me? And what about all the statements that God is love? What about Jesus' power to heal and to forgive? Isn't that something I should be able to *experience* as well as believe?

Gradually, the way I prayed began to change. Rather than just relying on the formal prayers I had learned in grade school, I began to sit in the chapel every evening and simply talk to Jesus. All I wanted was to feel his presence and to hear his still, small voice. I dusted off my Bible and began to read it slowly and prayerfully. And as my prayer changed, so too did my attitudes—again gradually, over time. Worries and concerns began to shrink. Guilt over past sins melted away. I began to feel a greater sense of freedom and hope, a sense that I could overcome sin and that I could get to know God in a deeper way.

This was all very new and exciting, but the most amazing part about it was how much life I began to find in the sacraments and the more traditional Catholic devotions. Attending Mass became more than a way of expressing my faith. It became a time to talk with Jesus, to hear his word to me, and to be filled with his presence. Confession remained an opportunity to get my sins off my chest, but it also became a time to encounter the mercy of a God who loved me completely and was deeply concerned about my life. The rosary became a chance to think and pray about Jesus' life and not just another way of praying for other people.

The Faith That Transforms

I could go on, but no matter what example I cite, I will always come back to the central reality that was unfolding for me: Jesus had become real to me, and in meeting him, I was being transformed.

This little bit of spiritual autobiography can serve as a good introduction to the book you are holding. In each chapter, *Taking It Personally* explores various doctrines and traditions of the Catholic faith through the lens of personal experience. Rather than try to teach about these topics, we want to share how they can empower us to live a new life. Rather than present a series of practices we *should* take up if we want to be better Christians, we want to talk about the power of the Holy Spirit to fill our hearts with a *desire* to draw closer to God through prayer, Scripture reading, and the Eucharist. And rather than talk about our moral and religious obligations to God, we want to emphasize God's passionate commitment to us: to redeem us, to pour his Spirit into us, and to glorify us in heaven. In short, we want to talk about how God wants to breathe life into us as we explore the truths of the gospel.

At the heart of all of these chapters is the conviction that living as Catholics is not completely up to us. If we want to see our faith take root and change the way we live, much of the work must be done by God. Only he can impart divine grace. Only he can melt hardened hearts. Only he can convince us of his love and show us his mercy. But here is where we come full circle: for any of this to happen, it is up to us to learn the art and science of prayer. We need to quiet our hearts and yield to our Father in faith and trust. And when we do, that's when real change begins. It happened to me during my college years, and it can happen to you.

So as you begin this book, ask the Lord to give you an open heart and mind. Take a step in faith and believe that your heavenly Father loves you unconditionally and wants to bless you abundantly. Know in your heart that you can experience his love and his life. As your faith becomes more personal, I pray that you will be transformed and become an ever-brighter reflection of God's love in the world.

CHAPTER 1

THE MYSTERY OF CONVERSION

To take our faith personally—to have a personal relationship with Jesus that allows us to be transformed into his image—usually begins with a conversion experience. At some point, we need to be touched by God's love, to accept that he died to save us, and to embrace his invitation to live with him forever. At the heart of every conversion is a strong desire to love God in return by giving our lives to him, by embarking upon a new journey that leads to a fulfilling faith life.

We all know of famous men and women who were turned around by an experience of conversion and who were set on a new course in life. These great saints dedicated themselves to loving and serving God with their whole heart, mind, and soul. We have only to think of St. Paul and St. Augustine, or St. Faustina and St. Edith Stein to see the witness of people whose lives took one-hundred-and-eighty-degree turns after they met the living God.

How about you? Have you had some kind of a conversion experience? Some people can point to a specific moment in their lives when God touched them deeply, and they committed their lives to him. Others can detect an ongoing pattern of conversion, where over months and years they have gradually grown closer to God. The truth is that God wants all of us to experience conversion, both initially and on an ongoing basis. Why? Because conversion is the beginning of the transformation process. Because it's through conversion that we begin to take our faith "personally" and let the Holy Spirit shape us into the image of Christ.

So how does conversion work? What is the interplay between God's power and our free choice? Why might a good and upright person still need conversion? And what comes after we've had a conversion experience? To answer these questions, let's look at several New Testament conversion stories—none as dramatic as St. Paul's, but all of them spiritual encounters with Christ that illustrate God's saving grace.

Initial Conversion: Our Choice and God's Grace

In Acts 16:11-15 Luke describes a Sabbath gathering of women outside the city of Philippi in Macedonia. Chief among them was a businesswoman named Lydia, a dealer of purple cloth. Because purple dye was the most costly to produce, it was typically reserved for only the finest fabrics, bought by wealthy customers. It took a lot of time and energy for a woman to be successful at that time in such a competitive business. Yet unlike her competitors, Lydia chose not to do business on the Sabbath day. She stepped away from the demands of her trade and spent time in worship with other women who knew about the God of the Old Testament. They had not yet heard about salvation through Jesus, but their love for God was strong and vibrant.

Led by the Holy Spirit

Before Luke mentions Lydia, he explains that the apostle Paul and his companions were led by the Holy Spirit to change their plans and extend their missionary trip into Macedonia. Their first stop was the city of Philippi, where they discovered the God-fearing women gathered by the river to celebrate the Sabbath.

Joining them in prayer, Paul found an opportunity to preach. Although we don't know exactly what he said, we can assume that it followed the pattern of other Pauline sermons: explaining who Jesus was, why he became a man, why he died and rose again, and maybe even what had happened to Paul when Jesus had revealed himself on the road to Damascus.

As Paul preached, the Holy Spirit came upon the women and opened Lydia's heart. God poured out a special grace of conversion. With his grace, God took Lydia's limited understanding and expanded it dramatically. On that day, she met Jesus and experienced the power of the Holy Spirit and the forgiveness of her sins. This was the beginning of the Philippian church—the first church in Europe.

The Story of Cornelius

The story of Cornelius in Acts 10 is another dramatic illustration of how deeply God wants to reach out to everyone. Cornelius was a gentile, a professional soldier stationed in Caesarea, the Roman capital of Palestine. Luke describes Cornelius and his whole family as being devout, generous with the poor, and God-fearing.

One day as Cornelius was praying, an angel appeared to him. Did God send this angel because he saw how spiritually hungry Cornelius was? Maybe. Was it because Cornelius showed such respect for his servants and cared for the poor? Maybe. After all, the angel said, "Your prayers and your alms have ascended as a memorial before God" (Acts 10:4). We really don't know. But we do know that, as in other stories in Scripture, Cornelius' story shows that the grace of God stands behind every conversion. The angel's appearance and message—that he should send for and listen to the apostle Peter—emphasizes that God will move at his own time and pace. This story also highlights an obvious reality: that our prayers and acts of love can help make us open to God when he is ready to act. It likewise highlights a remarkable mystery: it seems that through these very acts of prayer and love, we can move God to act.

Within twenty-four hours of Cornelius' vision, Peter had his own vision, which included a "feast" of animals deemed unfit for Jews to eat. Just as Peter was puzzling over this vision, a delegation from Cornelius arrived at his front door. When the men asked Peter to come with them, he felt the Holy Spirit moving him to accept their unusual invitation. (He probably needed this spiritual nudge before entrusting himself to a Roman soldier!)

Even though he didn't know what Peter was going to say, Cornelius was so enthused and expectant that he invited all his friends and relatives to come and listen. Cornelius reasoned that if the whole event had been engineered by an angel, something special must be on the way. Such an eager and open disposition gave God the freedom to work the miracle of conversion.

As Peter preached the gospel, the Spirit moved powerfully. Everyone in the house experienced the presence of God and turned their hearts to Jesus. Imagine Peter's surprise and joy when he saw these gentiles praising God and even speaking in tongues—just as he had experienced on the day of Pentecost!

Experience and Membership

All conversions are about experience and membership. For Cornelius and his family, the experience focused on a powerful outpouring of Jesus' love—an outpouring of grace and spiritual gifts that moved them to turn to the Lord in faith. And the membership was evident as Peter realized that even these gentiles were called to become members of the church.

Cornelius and his family received the Holy Spirit prior to any repentance on their part and prior to their baptism. This surprising sequence of events shows that there is no single set pattern for conversion. God works in many different ways. As far as he is concerned, the result—a faith-filled person who loves Jesus—is more important than the process.

Why did a good and holy family such as Cornelius' need to experience conversion? Because without Jesus, we really don't know the width, height, and depth of God's love. We don't know what it means to be reconciled to God. We don't know Eucharist and communion with Christ. We don't know Jesus as our Lord, our Savior, and our brother.

Based on what we know from Scripture, we might even say that

Cornelius and his family could have been saved without Peter. As Pope John Paul II said, "The mystery of salvation extends its boundaries beyond Christians." But God wants to give us so much more than an initial experience of salvation. He wants us to enjoy an intimate relationship with Jesus. He wants to shower us with all his promises and fill us with nothing less than divine life, in union with all the other members of the body of Christ.

This was the answer God gave to Cornelius and his family. Prior to Peter's arrival, they knew about God, but their knowledge was limited. They may even have had some spiritual experiences, but they were only partial. Likewise for us, we can have a relationship with Jesus and live in the Spirit each day, or we can settle for a limited version of everything that Jesus wants to give us.

A Threefold Process

In the stories of Lydia and Cornelius, Luke describes the way unbelievers joined the early church. For the first few centuries, the typical process was threefold. The order may be different today, but all three elements remain essential: *evangelization,* the sharing of the gospel; *conversion,* a decision to turn away from the world and to turn toward God; and *baptism,* the outpouring of God's grace to cleanse us from our sins and transform us into children of God and members of the church. Let's look at these three key elements.

Evangelization

Evangelization is the sharing of the "good news" about Jesus Christ, the Son of God who died to save us from our sins. The message of the gospel can come directly from the Holy Spirit, as it did for Paul (Acts 9:1-19), but the Holy Spirit usually speaks through someone who has already experienced conversion. In Lydia's case, the Spirit worked through Paul; in Cornelius' case, through Peter.

Whatever the source of the message, evangelization is always, first and foremost, a work of the Holy Spirit. Only he can pierce a person's heart with the promise of new life. Only he can reveal sin and pour out the healing love of the Father. Only he can open a person's heart—as he did for Lydia and Cornelius—and reveal Jesus. In short, only the Holy Spirit can "evangelize" a person in a way that leads to a true and life-changing conversion.

Conversion

There are two dimensions of conversion: initial conversion and ongoing conversion. In his parable of the prodigal son, Jesus illustrates both dimensions beautifully. Initial conversion—the primary decision to turn away from the world and to surrender one's life to Christ—is evident in the younger son, who "came to himself," abandoned his former way of life, and returned to his father's house (Luke 15:17). The older son, who was already living with his father, still needed to experience a deeper conversion—which we will discuss later in the chapter.

Both Lydia and Cornelius experienced an initial conversion because their hearts were open to the gospel message. They freely chose to reject and turn away from evil and to accept Jesus into their hearts. It was that initial choice—that initial conversion—that then set them on the path of discipleship.

Baptism

Baptism cleanses us of original sin, transforms us into a "new creation" (2 Corinthians 5:17), and incorporates us into the body of Christ (*Catechism of the Catholic Church,* 1262–70). Baptism supposes that a person has heard the gospel, has believed in Christ, and has confessed that Jesus is risen from the dead. In the case of infant baptism, it is assumed that the child's parents and godparents will undertake the primary responsibility of evangelizing that child and bringing him or her to a mature decision to turn from sin and turn to Christ.

After Lydia and Cornelius heard the gospel, they were baptized along with their whole households (Acts 10:48; 16:15). Their conversion—their decision to live for Christ—was sealed and empowered by the grace of God through this sacrament.

Ongoing Conversion: The Gospel of New Life

Conversion is a mysterious combination of God's all-powerful grace and our human decisions. We freely choose to give our lives to Jesus, but we would not even be able to make such a choice if it were not for the Holy Spirit's showing us our need for Christ and his great love for us. After our initial conversion, this same combination of grace and human choice continue to be necessary. We still need God's grace available to us in the Eucharist; we still need the wisdom of Scripture and the mercy available in the Sacrament of Reconciliation. Without all this grace, we are more likely to lose sight of Jesus and fall to temptation.

But beyond this generous supply of grace to support our initial conversion, God wants us to wake up every day and choose to enter the school of Christ, so that the Holy Spirit can continue to teach and train us. The Spirit wants to show us how to apply daily lessons of ongoing conversion to our lives so that we can come to see Jesus with unveiled faces—that is, with hearts that have been purified from all the residue of sin.

What Is Ongoing Conversion?

In initial conversion, we come to know Jesus and begin to experience the blessings of being members of his body, the church. Through conversion and baptism, we are brought into the kingdom of God and know that heaven is opened to us. Yet within each of us, pockets of behavior opposed to God remain and need to be eliminated—or, as St. Paul says, "put to death" (Colossians 3:5). These negative patterns of thought and action have the power to bind us up, lead to further sin, and separate us from Jesus and one another.

Ongoing conversion is the process of pursuing habits that lead to holiness and rooting out habits that separate us from Jesus. To get a better understanding of ongoing conversion, let's take a closer look at the older son in the parable of the prodigal son in Luke 15.

While the younger son left home and wasted his father's money on a sinful lifestyle, the older son stayed at home with the father. Unlike his brother, he remained a hard worker who never caused any trouble. Still, this older son revealed a jealous, selfish side when he saw how his father welcomed home his younger brother. For all his good qualities, this young man still had areas in his life that didn't fully reflect his father's kindness and generosity.

Let's assume for a moment that the older son kindly received the father's loving assurances. Let's assume that "grace" worked in his heart and opened his eyes. Perhaps he would have responded, "Father, I know that everything you have is mine. I see what you did for my brother, and I appreciate your love for him. Please forgive me for the way I acted when he came home. I let my self-righteousness get the best of me. I don't ever want to act that way again."

If this son had responded this way, he would have become "further converted." His old way of thinking and behaving would have been dealt another blow, and he would have experienced even more blessings living with his father.

Peter's Ongoing Conversion

Now let's return to the story of Cornelius for another look at ongoing conversion. As we continue to read along in Acts 10 and 11, we can see that God did not limit his work to Cornelius and his household. Just as he was pouring out his Spirit upon the gentiles, he was furthering Peter's ongoing conversion as well.

How? By expanding Peter's horizons and showing him that these gentiles were just as worthy of receiving salvation as the Jews were. In this "Second Pentecost," Peter saw gentiles—whom Jews had considered unclean and unworthy—filled with the power of the Holy Spirit, speaking in tongues and prophesying just as Peter and other apostles had done in Jerusalem on Pentecost. Here in far-off Caesarea, God revealed a plan to Peter that was far greater than Peter had known just moments earlier.

Peter first stepped out in faith when he went to see Cornelius. Then he took a larger step when he walked into Cornelius' house, since it was unlawful for a Jew to enter the home of a pagan. Then God asked Peter to take a giant step of faith and accept that even gentiles were redeemed by the cross of Christ and should be welcomed as members of the church.

Peter could accept this challenge because the Holy Spirit opened his eyes and helped him embrace the new path God was laying before him. In a similar way, God may seek to stretch our minds and unveil more of his plan of salvation to us.

As an example, consider the experience of Mark, a successful surgeon. Heading home from his office, Mark saw a homeless man begging near a street corner. Normally, Mark would have passed right by, but this time he gave the man some money. The man's life was in stark contrast to his own; he lingered in Mark's mind. Over the next months, Mark began to give more of his money, his time, and his heart to the poor. Within a year, he felt moved to reduce his medical practice and open a health clinic in a depressed part of town. Now, ten years later, Mark makes far less money than previously, but he doesn't really miss his old life. Whenever he reflects on all that has happened, Mark is amazed at how God used one encounter with a homeless man to set him on a new and unexpected path.

Three Decision-Making Scenarios

Ideally, all our decisions are made in response to the Holy Spirit's guidance and the teachings of Scripture and the church. Sometimes this decision-making process is simple and easy to adopt, making ongoing conversion almost natural.

However, there are other times when the issues are more complex, and we are not so sure about the right choice. These kinds of situations require a new light to go on in our minds, like a new revelation or an insight from another person. St. Peter had a few of these episodes, one of which is a classic example of a "gray area." After Jesus told the apostles that he was going to Jerusalem, where he would be put to death, Peter rebuked him: "God forbid it, Lord! This must never happen to you" (Matthew 16:22). Peter felt he was protecting his Master and trying to convince him not to follow a seemingly suicidal path. But Jesus shocked Peter by responding abruptly, "Get behind me, Satan!" (16:23). Even though Peter's intentions were good, his vision of what Jesus was supposed to do was faulty. We can reasonably imagine that when Jesus explained to Peter why his words and his thoughts were "of Satan," Peter understood and changed. This whole episode likely led Peter to a deeper conversion; he came to see how his words and intentions were in opposition to

God's plan of salvation and needed to be corrected.

There are other times when our own self-drive rises up in opposition to the Holy Spirit, and we knowingly act out of our selfishness. An example of this kind of situation—in which we know the right thing to do but fail to do it—is evident at the Last Supper. Jesus was saying good-bye to his closest friends and preparing them for his death. But instead of the sorrow or fear you might expect from them, the apostles argued about which of them was the greatest (Luke 22:21-24). They knew the right way, yet their self-centeredness got the better of them. We can assume that in time they too came to see why their behavior was opposed to God.

There are countless other stories of ongoing conversion in Scripture. Thomas had his doubts resolved. Job had his eyes opened. Isaiah had his sins cleansed. They all show us how much Jesus wants to give us the grace to draw closer to his love and power.

How to Deepen Your Conversion

How can we foster ongoing conversion? One way is through *recognition.* The Holy Spirit wants to teach us how to recognize the positive aspects of our lives and our behavior so that we can reinforce them. The Spirit also wants to help us recognize the negative elements and the way they cut us off from Jesus (John 16:8-11).

Sometimes the Spirit shows us personally what needs to change. It may happen when we're at Mass, in prayer, reading the Bible, or even as we're waking in the morning—any time at all. The Spirit may also use other people or situations to help us open our eyes.

Ongoing conversion is more likely to occur as we step back and *consider* why we do what we do—or why we did what we just did. What circumstances cause us to act in union with Jesus, and what circumstances cause us to act in opposition to him?

Take some time even today to review your actions. When you identify good behavior, thank Jesus and take steps to reinforce it. Should you see something negative, ask Jesus for the grace to work on it; identify practical steps you can take to help root it out of your life.

Finally, be sure to *guard your future*. Remember that Satan is always on the prowl (1 Peter 5:8), trying to convince us to stop checking our behavior or, worse, to let the negative aspects back into our lives. For this reason, we ask the Father to give us our daily bread, to lead us not into temptation, and to deliver us from evil.

Sometimes it seems that we will never graduate from the school of Christ, that there's always another area of our lives that needs our attention. But we should never get discouraged or think that our lives are reduced to fighting sin and trying to be perfect. As hard as it sometimes seems to be a Christian, every time we take another step closer to Jesus, he takes five steps closer to us. Jesus wants us to know that every time we take on habits and attitudes that enhance our new life, he transforms us a little more into his image.

If you are going to take your faith personally, then today and every day, tell yourself in prayer, "I want to live not for the world but for my Lord and Savior, Jesus Christ. I want to turn away from everything that is evil and toward everything that will open up the doors of grace and allow Jesus' light to shine upon me."

CHAPTER 2

PRAYER: THE TREASURE OF OUR LIVES

Imagine a married couple in love. Through their outward actions, they give the world glimpses of their love for each other: They spend time together; they smile at each other; they give up free time so that they can be with each other. These are but *signs* of their love. Their true relationship occurs deep within their hearts. Similarly, prayer is a relationship that occurs deep within our hearts. It may manifest itself in various actions, such as giving up time to pray and talk with God or keeping our hearts pure before him. Yet at its core, prayer is a *relationship*. And because prayer is a relationship, it has the power to change the way we think and act.

For centuries, God has been imploring his children to spend time with him in prayer, and people as diverse as powerful bishops and lowly peasants have responded to his call. And this is the wonder of prayer: God is inviting *all of us* to an intimate relationship with him, and *all of us* can respond by taking up a consistent prayer life.

Two telling gospel stories can give us valuable insights into prayer. Luke's account of Mary and Martha illustrates the importance of "sitting" at Jesus' feet. Another of Luke's stories, that of the repentant woman, teaches us to pour out our treasures before Jesus.

Sitting at Jesus' Feet

Mary's Better Part

One of the most moving gospel stories about the need for prayer is Luke's account of Martha and Mary (Luke 10:38-42). These two sisters lived with their brother, Lazarus, and Jesus had come to love them as his own family (John 11:1-3, 35-36). One day Jesus stopped by, and Martha invited him to stay for dinner. As Martha busied herself preparing the meal, Mary sat at Jesus' feet, soaking in his teaching. Growing agitated at Mary's apparent laziness, Martha blurted out, "Lord, do you not care that my sister has left me to serve alone? Tell her then to help me" (Luke 10:40). Jesus' response was far different from what Martha expected. "Martha, Martha, you are anxious and troubled about many things; one thing is needful. Mary has chosen the good portion, which shall not be taken away from her" (10:41-42).

Why did Jesus take such delight in Mary's approach to him? Because in Mary, Jesus found an open and humble heart to whom he could reveal his innermost thoughts and intentions. Free of the burdens and debates that he often faced with Pharisees and scribes, Jesus could speak as honestly with Mary as he did with the twelve apostles.

In her humble disposition and her willingness to learn from Jesus, Mary is a symbol of the church, the bride of Christ. How Jesus longs to see his church take Mary's place at his feet! He knows we can all be transformed as we fix our attention on him, both in quiet, personal prayer and in the corporate prayer of the liturgy. Like Mary, we can bring great joy to Jesus' heart. In fact, he delights in pouring out grace upon anyone who adopts a humble, teachable attitude.

Martha: Anxious and Concerned

Martha loved Jesus, too. Like her sister, she had come to believe in him and looked forward to whatever time he could spend with them. How was it possible, then, for her to have become so upset with Mary and to have missed out on the blessings of being at Jesus' feet?

Jesus could tell that Martha wasn't concerned only about the dinner. "Many things" were on her mind—so many anxieties and frustrations, in fact, that she couldn't recognize the heavenly reality in her midst. Just as Mary gives us one image of the church, so Martha provides another. Like Martha, we may be tempted to become preoccupied with the pressing needs the church faces. The poor and homeless cry out for help; many people have yet to hear the gospel; the sanctity of human life must be defended. We can become so busy trying to answer all these needs that we lose sight of the Master who longs to visit our home and give us a share in his heart.

To each of us, Jesus poses the question he asked Martha: "Are you so concerned with what must be done that you cannot simply sit with me? This is the 'one thing' that is 'needful.' This is the 'good portion' that will fill your heart with love for others. Without it, your service to me will end in frustration, bitterness, and emptiness." It's helpful to know that although so many racing thoughts clouded her mind, Martha eventually became a disciple ruled by the Spirit. The same can happen to us; Jesus never stops inviting people to sit with him.

"I Miss You"

When Fr. Mark first became a priest, he was so in love with Jesus that he spent hours in prayer every day. But once he became pastor of a large suburban parish, he felt crushed by the responsibility. On his best days, he spared only a little time to be with the Lord, and those times were dominated by pleas for financial help for the parish and fretting over the latest personality clashes within his church.

Gradually, one older woman noticed how tired Fr. Mark looked and how labored his homilies had become. She prayed for him, and, after a while, she approached him. "Fr. Mark," she said, "God told me to tell you something." Knowing she was a prayerful woman, he invited her into his office and listened intently. *Maybe God has finally answered my prayer for money.* What was the message? "Jesus wants you to know that he misses spending time with you."

Fr. Mark was stunned. With those few, simple words, he saw how distant he had grown from the Lord. He again set aside a few hours every morning to be with the Lord. He arranged to tend to his duties in the afternoons and evenings and delegated some of his tasks. Sure enough, the love that Fr. Mark had felt for Jesus in earlier years revived. What's more, some of the financial and relational problems in his parish diminished.

I miss you. How heartbreaking these words sound when spoken by God!

The Renewal of the Mind

At one time or another, many of us have felt especially aware of God's presence and love. It may have been at Mass or in the quiet of our bedroom, but no matter what the environment or the situation, God became very real to us. But after such a moving experience, the anxieties of life can easily cloud our memories and rob our peace.

Why is this? Often the problem is that while our hearts have been touched by God's love, often our minds still need renewal. And this can happen only by the power of the cross. As we sit at the feet of Jesus and gaze upon his cross, God will shine his light on the thoughts, desires, and assumptions within us that displease him. In the light of the love that Jesus poured out at Calvary, we will see our sin more clearly and begin to take on a new way of thinking and acting.

God wants to change our minds as we "fight the good fight of the faith" (1 Timothy 6:12) and gaze prayerfully upon the cross. Make no mistake: Such prayer is very difficult at times; it will require some sacrifice. But it is worth it, as the Lord exposes our old ways of thinking and replaces them with his way of mercy, compassion, and obedience.

What About You?

As she took Jesus' rebuke to heart, Martha's life was gradually changed. She came to acknowledge Jesus as "the Christ, the Son of God" and held firm trust in him even in the face of loss and sorrow

(John 11:22, 27). She continued to serve at her home (12:2), but freed from the anxiety and racing concerns that had previously dominated her thoughts. Over time, Martha learned to sit at Jesus' feet and hear from him.

Jesus is inviting all of us to sit before him. When we can't find the time to make it to Mass or to be alone with him, the Lord wants to say to us, "I really miss you. I want to reveal my heart to you." Jesus can be as present in our homes as he was in Martha's. Let's take the time to be with him and listen.

Sitting with Jesus in Prayer

Choose a time and a place.
- Make it a specific time dedicated only to payer—a time when you are alert and clear. (Psalm 92:1-2)
- Make sure it's a place where you are free from distraction and interruption. (Matthew 6:6)

Lay aside all other concerns.
- Examine your conscience and repent of your sins. (Psalm 130)
- Let God's mercy cleanse your conscience. (Romans 8:1-2)
- Put aside anxieties, problems, and struggles. (Hebrews 12:1-2)

Open your heart to the gospel. Consciously say yes to these truths each day:

- God created me out of love and loves me always. (1 John 4:10)
- God sent Jesus to give us life. (John 3:16)
- By his death and resurrection, Jesus conquered sin and death. (John 5:24)
- Jesus promised to be with us and to send the Holy Spirit. (John 14:15-16, 23)
- Jesus intercedes for us in heaven. (Hebrews 7:25)
- Jesus is coming again. (Matthew 16:27)

Praise God.

- Express your love and gratitude to your heavenly Father, to his Son Jesus, and to the Holy Spirit. (Psalms 95; 136; Hebrews 13:15; 1 Peter 2:9)
- Worship God honestly and from your heart. (Matthew 6:7-8)

Dwell in the presence of God.

- Listen actively to God in your heart as you read Scripture. (Isaiah 66:2)
- Sit quietly in God's presence and let his love touch your heart. (Psalm 131)

Intercede with faith and trust.
- Pray for the world, for the church, for your family, for your friends, and for yourself. (Matthew 7:7-11)

Write in your journal.
- What has God said to you?
- What do you want to carry into the day to keep your mind fixed on Jesus?
- What petitions will you keep close to your heart?

Placing Our Treasures at Jesus' Feet

Luke 7:36-50 tells the story of another woman drawn to Jesus, a woman known in town as a "sinner" and treated like an outcast—rejected, shunned, lonely. One day, Jesus, a rabbi and miracle worker, came to town. Itinerant preachers were not uncommon, but this one drew a huge crowd. He taught with authority; grace surrounded him; miracles flowed from his hands. For the first time in years, this woman was filled with hope. *Who is this man? I wonder if anyone else here feels the way I do?* As the gathering dispersed, she felt drawn to hear more from him and to speak to him herself.

Some time later, the woman heard that Jesus was visiting Simon, a local religious leader. She might have been filled with fear, knowing what Simon and his friends thought of her. But she mustered up the courage to burst into Simon's house and *throw* herself at Jesus' feet. Tears flooded her eyes—tears of sorrow over her sins and tears of joy in Jesus' presence. *This man knows all about me, but he doesn't draw back.*

It seemed as if no one else was in the room. This man loved her in a way no man ever had. She opened a flask of expensive ointment and poured it out on his feet. "What return can I give to the one who makes me feel so clean? I can give him my most precious treasure. Here, O Lord, is everything I own. I am happy to spend it on you."

Do I Need Jesus?

The woman's tears were in stark contrast to the reaction of Simon the Pharisee. He had invited Jesus, a fellow rabbi, into his home so that they could discuss their views. Unlike the woman, Simon did not feel any particular need for Jesus. So when Jesus entered the house, Simon neither embraced him nor extended the customary offer to wash his feet (Luke 7:44-45). He had heard many things about Jesus—both good and bad—and now he was going to test Jesus' fidelity to the Law of Moses.

While the woman wept at Jesus' feet, Simon saw his chance. Under Jewish law, a man became unclean through contact with a prostitute. But that didn't seem to bother Jesus; he was perfectly willing to let her touch him! Indignant, Simon discarded Jesus' prophetic preaching: "If this man were a prophet, he would have known . . . what sort of woman this is" (Luke 7:39).

Jesus summed up Simon's response in one sentence: "He who is forgiven little, loves little" (Luke 7:47). While this woman's encounter with Jesus resulted in the forgiveness of her many sins, Simon's heart was not changed. Because Simon could not see his own need for a savior, he could not understand the love this woman had for Jesus. The woman demonstrated what true faith is all about: heart-felt repentance, receiving forgiveness, worshipping Jesus, and giving him one's treasure—one's whole life.

Combining Faith and Prayer

Just as he touched the woman, Jesus wants to deepen our faith. For the sinful woman, approaching Jesus involved her whole being. Even though she had sinned greatly, at the moment when she came face-to-face with Jesus, she lived out the most important commandment: "You shall love the LORD your God with all your heart, and with all your soul, and with all your might" (Deuteronomy 6:5). This lifting up of our whole being in prayer is God's delight. Remember the prayer of Mary, the mother of Jesus: "My soul [my whole being] magnifies the Lord and my spirit rejoices in God my Savior" (Luke 1:46-47).

Such a prayer of yielding and vulnerability rises to the throne of heaven as a fragrant aroma of worship. In a story similar to Luke's account of the sinful woman, John 12:2-8 tells us that Martha's sister Mary herself took a pound of costly ointment and anointed Jesus' feet, wiping his feet with her hair. According to John, "the house was filled with the fragrance of the ointment" (12:3). When we lift our hearts and minds to God, the pleasing fragrance of our prayer rises to the throne of grace. "Through us God spreads the fragrance of the knowledge of him everywhere. For we are the aroma of Christ to God" (2 Corinthians 2:14-15).

Faith is the foundation from which this fragrant aroma rises. It is the foundation of prayer itself. The sinful woman had learned how to be intimate with her Lord. She could respond because she knew the Lord of love. She experienced the truth behind St. Paul's encouraging words, "By grace you have been saved through faith; and this is not your own doing, it is the gift of God" (Ephesians 2:8-9).

Prayer Is a Relationship

Throughout the centuries, many saints have taught their followers various methods of prayer. In our walk of faith, the Lord may have guided us into our own pattern or method of prayer. But whatever the method, prayer flows first and foremost from an inner relationship with the Holy Spirit. Through the Spirit dwelling in our hearts, Jesus' words become our own: "Thy kingdom come, thy will be done!" No matter how strong or weak they may feel, all Christians have the kingdom of God dwelling richly within them (see Luke 17:21). All Christians can receive the treasures of the kingdom of God and can come to know God intimately through a life of prayer.

Through prayer, our relationship with God can grow and mature. As we continue in prayer, we will sense the presence of the Lord more often. And his presence will lead us to deeper worship and love for God. Like the sinful woman who "wasted" her most prized possession on Jesus, we come before Jesus, weep over our sins and those of the world, and lay down all of our treasures before the Lord. Our treasures may include our reputation, our security, or our comfort. Whatever they are, we place them at Jesus' feet and we worship him.

Teach Us to Pray!

Like conversion, prayer is a gift from God. It is not something *we do* for him, but a beautiful gift *he bestows* on us as we humbly seek his presence. Having learned from this sinful woman, let us seek Jesus every day with the same love that compelled her. What a privilege to have wept before him in repentance and love! Yet we too can know this same privilege. We can love Jesus in spirit and truth because the Holy Spirit within us loves to spend time in God's presence. We can wait for Jesus in prayer. We can kneel at his feet and weep with love for the One who has so much love and mercy for us.

"Thank you, Jesus, for giving us your Spirit and inviting us into a relationship of love with you and your Father. Lord, teach us to pray."

CHAPTER 3

HEARING GOD'S VOICE IN A BUSY WORLD

Have you ever noticed how quickly people can react when the phone rings? Have you ever "dropped everything" to answer? Some calls are urgent. Others are simply invitations to chat. Whatever the purpose of the call, we want to ensure that we have the chance to respond. With the advent of answering machines, caller ID, and e-mail, we are nearly guaranteed not to miss a single message. If telephone calls from family and friends are so important to us, how much more so are the messages God wants to give us and the conversations he wants to have with us!

Many people have lost a sense that God wants to speak to them on a daily basis. Although many Christians know that they should pray, they may lack confidence that they can actually hear from God. In this chapter, we want to discuss aspects of the Holy Spirit's speaking to us. What is his message? How is that message communicated? How can we discern God's voice from that of others?

God Has a Message

Let's consider three types of messages God has for us. Some of God's calls are invitations to join him in unfolding his plan for the church. Others are directed toward a change he wants us to make. And sometimes God simply wants to comfort and encourage us.

An Invitation to Join In

A beautiful young girl was in love with a fine, upstanding man. A wedding date was set, and the preparations were underway. But suddenly, all the plans changed. Out of nowhere, the woman was asked to accept a new proposal: would she be willing to give up her plans and become the mother of God? Mary freely accepted God's call, even though she didn't know how this would happen (Luke 1:34). What's worse, she had to tell Joseph she was carrying a baby—conceived by the Holy Spirit.

Scripture tells us that Joseph didn't believe Mary at first. For all he knew, his bride-to-be had betrayed him. He decided to cancel the wedding as quietly as possible (Matthew 1:19). But everything changed for Joseph when a dream convinced him that Mary's words were true. In the end, Joseph married Mary and accepted this child as his own.

God called Mary and Joseph, and both of them said yes. Their call was extraordinary. But even today, as in every age, God invites his children to play a part in his unfolding plan for all humanity. Even today we can sense the voice of God. We can come to know his agenda and learn how to sense what he wants us to do as we work with him to bring his plan to completion. God truly wants each of us to be open to his Spirit and to say yes to his call.

A Call to Change

When asking us to change our ways, God sometimes speaks to us directly, as he did when he told Paul to stop persecuting and start serving him, or when he told Francis of Assisi to go and rebuild his church, or when he told Catherine of Siena to leave the comfort of her home to go preach and heal throughout Italy.

At other times, God encourages us to make a change through the voice of another person. Remember the story of David and Nathan? To cover his adultery with Bathsheba, David plotted to have her soldier-husband Uriah killed in battle. The plan worked: Uriah was dead, and Bathsheba was free to marry David. No one suspected, until God sent the prophet Nathan to confront David's sin. At Nathan's words, David's eyes were opened, and he confessed, "I have sinned against the LORD" (2 Samuel 12:13). Just as God used Nathan to speak to David, he will use people in our lives—family members, friends, co-workers, or fellow parishioners—to speak his word to us.

But sometimes God speaks in more subtle ways. One woman wanted to keep her marriage together, but anything she tried seemed to make matters worse. She and her husband were moving toward a permanent separation. As a last-ditch effort, she decided to stop trying anything new, except that she would go to Mass each morning and stay after for a few minutes to ask Jesus for help.

In a few weeks, her husband asked, "What's gotten into you? You seem happier and more content. Are you reading another one of those self-help books?" The woman hadn't been aware that she had changed. But upon further reflection, she could see that she had become more peaceful; she smiled more easily. Where previously she had been aloof, she was more now more affectionate toward her husband. All she had done was ask Jesus for help, and her outlook improved.

The changes he saw convinced her husband to go to Mass with

her and begin praying. Two years later, the man and woman are still together and are building a strong, God-centered marriage.

Did God specifically tell this woman to go to church and pray each day? Or was it her own decision? Did God make her more attractive to her husband? Even the wife herself can't be sure. But she does know that something inside led her to cry out to God, and that changes in her life affected her husband. The woman is convinced that her marriage was saved because God led her down a new path and she chose to follow him.

A Call of Encouragement

Who can forget the story of the Israelites wandering, hungry and thirsty, in the desert? Although they had seen God deliver them from Pharaoh, they began to believe that they would be better off back in Egypt. God heard their complaints, but he didn't punish them. Instead, he gave them water, manna, and quail. Just as God encouraged the Israelites, he wants to encourage us.

God also gave Elijah heavenly encouragement when he was trying his best to do the Lord's work under the threat of a royal death warrant. On the run, depressed and miserable, Elijah lay down under a tree and told God he wanted to die (1 Kings 19:4). An angel of the Lord told the sleeping Elijah that he was not going to die; God had much more for him to do. Pointing to some food and water that had miraculously appeared, the angel said, "Get up and eat, otherwise the journey will be too much for you" (19:7). Just as God encouraged and fed Elijah, Jesus wants to give us his encouragement and feed us with his own living bread in the Eucharist.

When our primary goal in prayer is developing a relationship with Jesus, anything can happen. Some people have sensed Jesus smiling at them, holding their hands, or putting his arm around their shoulders. Some have experienced a powerful rush of love from their heavenly Father. Others have been renewed with hope and strength. Some come to a new understanding of the Eucharist.

Responding to God

As Christians in a fast-paced world, we face a great challenge. We have to learn how to "keep up" and still be quiet enough to hear God's call for our lives, our families, and his church.

God doesn't want us to ignore our goals and plans. But at the same time, he does want us to make Jesus our first priority. He wants to teach us how to balance our hopes and dreams with his desire to usher in his kingdom. He knows that if we let our own goals and dreams completely dominate our attention, we'll find it hard to listen for his words of direction and encouragement.

Every day, make a point of talking to God. Tell him how much you love him. Tell him all about your plans and your dreams. Imagine him listening to you intently, his heart filled with love and compassion. Then ask God what he wants to say to you. Ask him to share with you his dreams and plans for you and for his church. Even if you don't think you're hearing anything, keep trying.

Melanie: "How I Heard the Lord"

When I got the news earlier this year that Dan, my husband, had cancer, I felt as if I couldn't even breathe. . . . In the middle of a desperate prayer, a Scripture passage came into my mind, something like this: "Don't fear anything that can harm the body but not the soul." I repeated these words out loud, and my tears and fears subsided. My breathing returned to normal.

The words didn't tell me that Dan would be okay or even that he wouldn't die. But they did tell me that Dan's spirit wouldn't be harmed. As I kept repeating the words, I felt God reassuring me that cancer couldn't harm what was most important—Dan's soul. When I got home, I found the Bible passage, in Luke 12:4. A few verses later, Jesus said, "Are not five sparrows sold for two pennies? And not one of them is forgotten before God. Why, even the hairs of your head are all numbered" (12:6-7). From that moment on, I knew I could entrust Dan to God. He knew Dan intimately and cared for him deeply.

Dan's surgery went well; the doctors are encouraged. I still get occasional moments of fear, but every time, I know I can turn to this passage and hear God's comforting voice.

God Has a Voice

In his late teens, when Richard started smoking, there were no surgeon general's warnings, no studies, and no bad press about tobacco. He'd been a pack-a-day smoker for close to twenty years when researchers first issued warnings about the link between cigarette smoking and lung disease.

These disturbing findings bothered Richard's wife. She gathered and presented him with information and asked him to quit smoking—for his sake as well as their children's. Richard appreciated her concern, but said that he just couldn't stop. Besides, were the studies really conclusive?

Months later, a co-worker, diagnosed with cancer, had a lung removed. Shaken, Richard asked his doctor for a checkup. Though tests were clean, the doctor urged him to quit smoking. The next year, Richard's brother bet him fifty dollars that he couldn't quit smoking for six months. Richard accepted the challenge and won the bet. Happily, he pocketed the money, but he was smoking again within two weeks.

Two more years passed. At his annual checkup, X-rays showed a spot on his lung. "It could be nothing," the doctor said, "or it could be a sign of worse things to come. You can't play games anymore. You've got to quit." From that moment twelve years ago, Richard has not had a single cigarette. Richard's story illustrates how deeply God wants to talk to us—and all the different means he will use to get our attention.

A "Still Small Voice"

How does God speak to us? More often than not, it won't be in dramatic ways, but in the ordinary, everyday rhythms of our lives. He may speak through a spouse, a book, a friend, a homily, or a setting sun. Or we may hear him as we seek him in quiet prayer, as we receive the Eucharist, as we read the Bible (aspects of the Christian life discussed in other chapters). Let's look at Elijah again to gain more insight into hearing and recognizing God's voice.

Fleeing the murderous Queen Jezebel, Elijah headed for a certain mountain, where he knew that God would speak to him. When he got there, Elijah felt a mighty wind sweeping by, but the Lord wasn't in the wind. He felt the mountain move, but the Lord wasn't in the earthquake. Fire fell around him, but the Lord wasn't in the fire. Finally, Elijah heard a gentle whisper, and he knew that this was God (1 Kings 19:11-13).

Was this "still small voice" something Elijah heard with his ears, or was it something Elijah sensed in his heart? We don't really know, and, in one sense, it's not important. What matters is that Elijah was able to sense the presence of God, "hear" his voice, and respond to him. The promise of the gospel is that because the Holy Spirit lives in us, we can all learn to become as sensitive to God's voice as Elijah was. We really can hear the Lord!

Enlivening Our Spirits

Because we are made in the image of God, we have the ability to understand things on a natural level and on a spiritual level. We have the ability to be intuitive, to imagine, to reason, to remember, and to make choices. But each of these abilities has a spiritual dimension as well as a natural dimension. This spiritual dimension comes to life when we are baptized, and it grows as we draw closer to Jesus through prayer.

Ideally, the natural and the spiritual dimensions should work together to help us live peaceful and fruitful lives. But experience tells us that we tend to let the natural dimension dominate our thoughts and actions. We end up placing more trust in ourselves than we place in God.

St. Thomas Aquinas noted that it can be difficult to tell whether a thought or an intuition comes from the Holy Spirit or from our own minds. Distinguishing between the natural and the spiritual takes practice, testing, and review.

This can sound intimidating, but it's also true that with even a little practice, we can begin to take on the mind of Christ (1 Corinthians 2:16). Pope John XXIII often mentioned how he felt inspired by the Holy Spirit to initiate Vatican II. Was this inspiration a clear message from God, a sense John XXIII had in his heart, or a good idea he came up with on his own? It's hard to tell, but hindsight indicates that Vatican II was one of the most important works of God in the twentieth century.

Mother Teresa said that God moved her to leave her teaching job and ultimately form a new religious order. God placed in her heart a calling to care for the "poorest of the poor." Did she receive this calling in prayer? In a dream? Through the words of another person, or as she reflected on her prior experiences? The method God uses doesn't really matter. What is important is that Mother Teresa was receptive to his call. And we know that as God's obedient servant, Mother Teresa was able to influence the whole world.

Just as he did for Mother Teresa and Pope John XXIII, the Lord stands at the door of our hearts. He promises that if we open the door to him, he will come in and eat with us (Revelation 3:20). He will enable us to sense his love and his compassion. He will fill our minds with his truth, and he will help give our lives direction and purpose. Who knows? We may make an impact as strong as that of the greatest saints. We may find the grace to bring much-needed peace into our homes or neighborhoods or to serve the poor and needy.

Called to Build the Kingdom

The "still small voice" that Elijah heard directed him to anoint Elisha as his successor. What might have happened if Elijah hadn't heard or chosen to obey? What would have come of God's plan for Elisha to serve the Israelites?

Similarly, Scripture tells us that Peter, James, and John, Jesus' three closest disciples, could often be selfish, proud, narrow minded, and weak in their understanding of God's will. Yet over time and with the help of the Holy Spirit, they learned to develop their spiritual senses and to hear God's voice. Both natural and spiritual dimensions began to work together more closely, and Peter, James, and John became builders of the early church.

As noted earlier, God's message to us often shows us the part he wants us to play in the building of his kingdom on earth. If you begin to seek Jesus on a regular basis—to open the door of your heart— you will find the Holy Spirit strengthening your spiritual senses with deeper faith and a greater ability to hear God's voice. He will shower you with revelation about the wisdom and love of God (1 Corinthians 2:9-10).

As a result, you will grow in your ability to understand the calling that God has for your life. You will think more like Jesus and make your decisions more in light of the Holy Spirit's leading. You will learn how the natural and the spiritual work together, and you will see God leading you to fulfill his purposes.

Phil: "How I Heard the Lord"

As a young man, I was attracted to a girl who had moved into my neighborhood. We got to know each other and had a lot in common. We dated and met each other's parents, and everything was great. But around the time I started looking at rings, I was overcome with doubts. It was a typical case of the jitters, but it caught me off guard. What if she said no? Who was I kidding to think I was good enough for her?

My best friend and I met for lunch. When I told him what I was thinking, he laughed. He knew that I loved this woman and that she loved me; he sensed that we would be happy together. "Why do you have to complicate things so much?" he asked. "Can't you believe that God wants to give you something good?"

Those few, simple words cut me to the heart and calmed my fears. I'm convinced that the Holy Spirit used my friend's words to give me the boost I needed. I'm convinced that God wants to speak to us through good friends.

Distinguishing God's Voice

Just as children have a natural ability to recognize their parents' voices and equate them with love and security, we all have a spiritual ability to recognize God's voice and the comfort of his presence. In the parable of the good shepherd, Jesus tells us that his children—his "sheep"—can distinguish his voice from others (John 10:1-18).

"That's All There Is to It"

In a workshop for young hopefuls, a professional basketball player explained how to make a long shot: "Keep your eyes on the basket. Visualize the shot in your mind. Then take the shot. That's all there is to it."

Now, this basketball player had put in thousands of hours of practice. Making a long shot had become almost second nature for him. His students, however, had far less experience. They had much to learn before they could say, "That's all there is to it."

Likewise, it would be unreasonable for us to think that we can recognize the voice of God with little effort. It takes practice, experimentation, patience, and creativity. Prayer is an art as well as a science. It's not something we can simply read about and expect to accomplish perfectly at our first attempt. Each of us has to find the best way to pray and hear from Jesus.

There are many ways to pray, including traditional formal prayers, intercessory prayers, meditative prayers, centering prayers, praying the psalms, singing hymns, and spontaneous vocal prayers. Whatever the method, prayer means talking to and listening to Jesus. It means opening our hearts to him and asking him to reveal to us his love and will. It means telling him about our hopes and dreams, our hurts and fears; and it means asking him for his forgiveness, direction, and wisdom. When this is at the heart of our prayer, we can be sure that we will come to know God's voice intimately. And knowing his voice will heal and change our hearts.

Identifying Other Voices

Jesus is our good shepherd, but he knows that it's up to us to decide which voices we will listen to. We all are aware of other voices that seek to drown out the voice of the Lord. Let's look at four sources of these "voices": the devil, our own selfish concerns, memories of past hurts, and the false wisdom of the world. Jesus wants us to distinguish these voices from his and learn how to seek his protection and guidance. Future chapters will discuss in more depth how to distinguish these false voices from God's voice.

Test the Message

There's no doubt about it: prayer takes time and effort. But with ongoing experimentation and commitment to some "trial and error" sessions, we can learn how to sense the voice of the Lord. There is no magic formula. We've got to do some work to make prayer fruitful.

If the thoughts that come to us in prayer move us to greater love, compassion, forgiveness, or generosity, we can be pretty confident that God is behind them. Remember: the devil is the "accuser" (Revelation 12:10), and the Holy Spirit is your "counselor," "comforter," and "advocate" (John 14:16).

Scripture tells us to "test everything" and "hold fast to what is good" (1 Thessalonians 5:21). Whenever you sense God saying something to you, write it down in a prayer journal. Examine it. Question it. Use common sense and good reasoning to understand how you should put it into practice. If you sense that the message pertains to something very important or a major decision, consult with your spouse, parents, pastor, or someone else who can help you discern what you are hearing.

Though prayer is a learning process, we can all be encouraged to know that God wants to give us all "a spirit of wisdom and revelation" so that we might know him better (Ephesians 1:17). All of us can become "masters" of prayer over time. It just takes a little discipline, a lot of faith, and a good amount of trust in God's goodness and in his desire to speak to us.

CHAPTER 4

SCRIPTURE: GOD SPEAKS TO HIS CHILDREN

In a friend's garden one day, the man who would become St. Augustine heard a child's voice say, "Take and read." Seeing a Bible nearby, he opened it. In Scripture, Augustine heard the Lord speaking to him; from that moment, his life changed.

How the Lord longs to speak to our hearts and convince us of his love! His word can bring us wisdom and direction, healing and freedom, far beyond anything we can ask or imagine.

In this chapter, we'll take a historical look at Jesus' knowledge and use of the Hebrew Scriptures. We'll then introduce study and interpretation methods that can help readers plumb the depths of Scripture. And finally, we will discuss an early Christian model by which Scripture reading and prayer can become a conversation with God.

Formed by the Word

If we read the gospels in one way, we might come away with the impression that Jesus simply appeared on the scene after his baptism, having been infused with divine wisdom to preach the gospel. Yet a closer look, especially at the beginnings of Matthew and

Luke, reminds us that Jesus spent his first thirty years on earth living quietly and drinking deeply of the faith of his ancestors. Even as he learned the trade of carpentry from Joseph, Jesus immersed himself in the word of God and allowed that word to form him.

How would a young Jewish man in first-century Palestine have learned Scripture? What were the synagogue services like? What passages were frequently read and discussed? In considering these questions, we can glimpse how God's word had become a part of Jesus' character as he grew in wisdom and the grace of God (see Luke 2:40, 52). In his love for Scripture, Jesus—fully human as well as almighty God—shows us how powerful God's word can be in teaching us, comforting us, and forming us as his people.

Jesus and the Old Testament

Hand-copied scrolls containing the Hebrew Scriptures were so expensive that a village synagogue like that in Nazareth might not have owned a complete set. But regular Sabbath prayer services would have required copies of the texts of the Torah (the Pentateuch or Law), the Prophets (including the Books of Samuel and Kings), and the Psalms.

Mary and Joseph would have taken Jesus to the synagogue service every Sabbath. What's more, if Mary had indeed been raised in the temple from the age of three until her marriage to Joseph—as ancient tradition holds—we can imagine her attending the temple liturgies and learning the Hebrew Bible herself. You might imagine her teaching her son at home, telling him about the destiny of the

Jewish people, about God's faithfulness to his promises, and about the coming Messiah. Such a prayerful environment was fertile ground in which the seed of Scripture could take deep root.

Synagogue Service and Readings

Synagogues originated in Palestine after the fifth century B.C., to establish a place in every town where the Jews could meet together to pray and study Scripture. We don't know precisely what a synagogue service looked like in the first century, but we can gain some insights from biblical and nonbiblical sources.

Sabbath morning services began with a prayer under the leadership of a "president of the assembly" and an assistant. Of Judaism's famous Eighteen Blessings, three were recited at the beginning of the service and three toward the end. The assistant recited the *Shema Israel*, the fundamental text of Israel's faith (Deuteronomy 6:4-9), and several lectors read from the Scriptures. After the readings, someone chosen by the president gave a homily. A psalm was sung, a collection was taken up for the poor, and the service ended with a final blessing by the leader of the congregation.

What specific passages might a Jew of Jesus' time have heard most frequently? In the Book of Acts, Luke says that Paul and his companions went to the Antioch synagogue. "After the reading of the law and the prophets, the rulers of the synagogue" told Paul and the others, "If you have any word of exhortation for the people, say it" (13:15). This combination—Pentateuch, Prophets, and sermon—is also found in 2 Maccabees 15:9.

Lists of Sabbath synagogue readings compiled around A.D. 200 show the Pentateuch and Prophets divided into a three-year cycle of approximately 150 sections, about 50 per year, one for each non-feast-day Sabbath. The Pentateuch was the centerpiece, read in continuation. Texts from the Prophets illustrated and complemented the main lesson.

Assuming these lectionary readings were in use at the time of Jesus—at least in a basic format—we can imagine which texts young Jesus heard again and again. We can imagine passages that might have left a deep impression on him as he came to understand who he was and what God had called him to do. For instance, the story of the six days of creation in Genesis 1:1–2:4 was paired with the prophecy about the new heaven and new earth in Isaiah 65:17-25. The story of Adam and Eve—including their fall into sin—was paired with the promise of salvation in Isaiah 51:6-16.

This constant rhythm of event and fulfillment, of foreshadow and promise, must have filled Jesus' heart. Picture him pondering these and similar texts, and in his human nature gradually realizing that he was the Messiah, the "child born to us"—the Son of God, with an authority greater than that of Moses. Imagine him learning that he was the one destined to fulfill the greatest promises God had ever made to his people. How his heart must have thrilled, even as he wondered at how all of this might take place.

The Word Transformed

Jesus' reliance on the Hebrew Scriptures is evident throughout the gospels. When he entered into his ministry, he was quickly recognized as one who spoke "with authority" (Luke 4:32), because both in his words and his actions he transformed the meaning of Scripture. In the Sermon on the Mount, for example, Jesus challenged a superficial reading of Pentateuch passages as he taught how God wants to write his law on our hearts: "You have heard that it was said . . . 'You shall not kill.' . . . but I say to you that every one who is angry with his brother shall be liable to judgment" (Matthew 5:21-22). "You have heard that it was said, 'You shall not commit adultery.' But I say to you that every one who looks at a woman lustfully has already committed adultery with her in his heart" (5:27-28).

But Scripture was more than the starting point for Jesus' sermons. When he was undergoing personal attack, he let God's word be his sole defense. Facing accusations for eating with sinners, Jesus quoted the prophet Hosea: "I desire mercy, and not sacrifice" (Matthew 9:10-13; Hosea 6:6). As he drove marketers from the temple, he stitched together Isaiah and Jeremiah: "Is it not written, 'My house shall be called a house of prayer for all the nations,' but you have made it a den of robbers" (Mark 11:17; Isaiah 56:7; Jeremiah 7:11).

Even more telling was Jesus' reliance on God's word in times of crisis. During his forty days in the desert, Jesus turned to Scripture to refute the devil's temptations (Matthew 4:1-11). At his arrest, when his friends were about to desert him, Jesus recognized that it must be this way to fulfill Scripture (Mark 14:49). Finally, we see

Jesus' love for God's word as he hung on the cross, when he turned to the psalms "My God, my God, why have you forsaken me?" (Mark 15:34; Psalm 22:1) and "Father, into your hands I commit my spirit!" (Luke 23:46; Psalm 31:5).

The Word in Our Hearts

It is clear that, like Ezekiel before him, Jesus had digested God's word (Ezekiel 3:1). Scripture had become such a part of Jesus' personality that he could not help but draw from it as he sought to live in his Father's presence. He had allowed the word of God to be so impressed on his heart that it became the basis for all his actions and thoughts. In Jesus, more than in anyone else, the words of the psalmist are fulfilled: "I will never forget your precepts; for by them you have given me life. . . . Great peace have those who love your law; nothing can make them stumble" (Psalm 119:93, 165).

Keys to Reading Scripture

Imagine a recent acquaintance sitting down with you and perusing your high school yearbook. The pictures would conjure a host of memories for you—people and events connected with your youth. Your acquaintance, however, would not share in those memories; he would see pictures of someone else's past, not connected to his experience.

It is similar with Scripture. If you approach a passage without much understanding of the sweep of salvation history and life in biblical times, you might not be able to grasp much beyond the surface of a person's words or a sequence of events. The deeper our understanding, the greater our appreciation will be. As illustrated in Jesus' parable of the sower and the seed (Luke 8:5-15), our hearts and minds can become fertile soil in which the seed of God's word can sprout and bear fruit that yields a hundredfold.

Scripture is meant to be the heart of our faith, and yet questions of interpretation have haunted virtually every generation. Even Jesus' first disciples needed him to interpret or "open their minds to" Scripture (Luke 24:45; see 24:31-32). In John's gospel, only after Jesus had risen and breathed the Holy Spirit upon them did the disciples truly understand and believe his words (John 2:22; 14:26).

To help believers in our age come to a clearer grasp of Scripture and open their hearts more fully to the Spirit, the Pontifical Biblical Commission (PBC) issued a document, *The Interpretation of the Bible in the Church,* to guide us in the way we read and reflect upon Scripture. Here we summarize some of this document.

Forms, Sources, and Versions

Because the Bible is filled with different types of literature, and because it developed over more than two thousand years, we need to use a variety of methods to plumb its depths. In its first section, the PBC document analyzes methods and provides guidance in how they should be used.

One method—*source criticism*—seeks to discover the sources behind a text. For example, most scholars suggest that the gospels of Matthew and Luke drew significantly from two earlier sources: the gospel of Mark and a collection of Jesus' sayings commonly referred to as "Q."

Another method—*redaction criticism*—studies how the various authors edited or "redacted" these sources as they sought to explain God's work to their specific audience. Compare the two versions of the Our Father, found in Luke 11:2-4 and in Matthew 6:9-13. Compared to Luke, Matthew's gospel contains an expanded version of Jesus' prayer. Both Evangelists include the petition "your kingdom come," but Matthew's version includes the explanatory phrase "your will be done." God's kingdom is present whenever his will is done on earth as faithfully as it is done in heaven. Similarly, Matthew adds a prayer for deliverance from the evil one to the prayer for rescue from the time of trial. At times of great trial, it is the evil one who tries to lead believers to give up their faith. It seems that both Evangelists drew from the traditions and sources that described Jesus' prayer; each evangelist shaped the traditions to reflect a different aspect of the same truth of the privilege of praying to God as our good and loving Father.

Yet another method is called *form criticism*. If we were to read a newspaper editorial page looking for an unbiased account of the news, we would be misinterpreting the purpose of editorials. If we were to read the comics pages in search of hard facts, we would end up with a very strange view of the world. Similarly, to interpret the Book of Jonah properly, we need to know its form. If we view it as a historical account in the strict sense, we might feel compelled to investigate how long a human being can survive for three days inside a huge fish. But if we identify the form as a parable—a more correct view—our interpretation will have stronger implications for us. Like Jonah, we can try to avoid God's call to proclaim his mercy.

While recognizing how valuable these methods can be, the PBC also acknowledged their limitations. By placing a passage within its historical context and leaving it there, we can distance ourselves from the text and thereby limit its ability to speak to us. For instance, the Song of Songs is a set of poems celebrating married love, yet through the ongoing guidance of the Spirit, both Jews and Christians have seen in these poems an expression of the intimate relationship between God and his people. Imagine how much insight we would lose if we looked at this book only for guidance in marriage!

The Literal and the Spiritual

The PBC document goes on to show some of the many ways Scripture can speak to its readers. As the inspired word of God, the Bible has both a literal and a spiritual meaning. The "literal" sense refers to the human author's original intentions and goals in writing a specific book or passage. The "spiritual" sense refers to the Holy Spirit's purpose in inspiring the human author to write as he or she did. Although these two senses are not always different from each other, there is a way that the fullness of the Spirit's purposes in any given passage can escape the recognition of the original, human author.

For example, the young woman or "virgin" referred to in Isaiah's Emmanuel prophecy (Isaiah 7:14) can be understood in two senses. According to the literal sense—what the prophet intended around the year 734 B.C.—the words probably referred to the wife of King Ahaz and their son, Hezekiah, who was a just and God-fearing king. According to the spiritual sense, however, the prophecy refers ultimately to Mary, the virgin who bore the Son of God in the flesh (Matthew 1:22-23). This distinction between the spiritual and the literal sense emphasizes how important it is to approach God's word with open hearts and ask the Spirit to deepen our understanding and lead us to a greater love for God and his people.

The Interpretation of the Bible in the Church calls us all to a deeper dedication to study the word of God and accept it as God's revelation. Studying the history and culture behind the very diverse books of the Bible can open up new dimensions of understanding. Approaching the Bible as a story can help us discover our own story within the biblical story. In all these ways, our use of Scripture in prayer and at Mass can become even more enriching.

A Conversation with God

Scripture is not simply a collection of words to be read, however wise or moving these words may be. Scripture is the word of God— his voice speaking intimately to us, refreshing us and teaching us. As the Fathers of the Second Vatican Council pointed out, "In the sacred books, the Father who is in heaven comes lovingly to meet his children, and talks with them" (*Dogmatic Constitution on Divine Revelation,* 21).

The challenge we face is in allowing the words on the page to have an impact on our hearts. God our Father longs to teach us and form us, and he does this as we open our hearts to and respond to his word.

Lectio Divina: Reading the Scriptures in Faith

Tradition provides a way of reading Scripture—known as *lectio divina* or inspired reading—by which God's word can change our hearts. In its truest sense, *lectio divina* is meant to draw us from the word of God in Scripture to God the Word—Jesus himself, who gives us a share in his wisdom and love. *Lectio divina* involves four steps: reading, meditation, prayer, and contemplation. Guigo the Carthusian, a spiritual writer from the Middle Ages, described these steps:

> Reading is the careful study of the Scriptures, concentrating all one's powers on it. Meditation is the busy application of the mind to seek, with the help of one's own reason, for knowledge of hidden truth. Prayer is the heart's devoted turning to God to drive away evil and obtain what is good. Contemplation is when the mind is in some sort lifted up to God. . . . Seek in reading and you will find in meditating; knock in mental prayer and it will be opened to you by contemplation. (see *CCC,* 2654)

Reading and Meditation: The Words of Scripture

Reading and meditation focus on the actual words of Scripture and their meaning. Reading involves understanding what the passage says. Read the passage carefully a couple of times. Try reading it aloud, paying attention to the way the words should be spoken. You might outline the main points or try to put the passage into your own words. Ask who is speaking to whom. Why? What are the main events or facts being communicated? What is the context of the passage? What situation gave rise to these words? Resources such as commentaries, Bible dictionaries, or other study guides can reveal more dimensions of the rich tapestry that is God's word. The challenge in this stage is to remain focused on the words themselves, even if referencing other works about the word of God.

In meditation, we move beyond what the passage says to uncover what it means. We move from the "then" of history to the "now" of our lives. In this stage, try to focus on a word or a phrase that strikes you, and ponder that particular part of the passage quietly and peacefully. Open your mind to the Spirit and the heavenly dimension of the words. Allow them to speak to your own situation, to challenge or comfort you, to move you to repentance or praise. That way, the immediate words you read can give way to the timeless truths of the gospel that give life.

Prayer and Contemplation: The Word in Our Hearts

The promise of studying Scripture is that our study does not end with the efforts of our human intellect. In prayer and contemplation, the focus moves from the words of God to Jesus himself. God's word is not only the written word in Scripture, but the very person of Jesus, the Word made flesh (John 1:14).

In prayer we respond to the word of God, asking the Spirit to write these words on our hearts. As God's children, we have freedom to pray simply and spontaneously, whether that means singing, asking God questions, or just worshipping him for his goodness and perfection. We can confess our sins to the Lord and ask him to give us the grace to live in greater faithfulness to his word. In prayer we begin a heartfelt conversation with our heavenly Father. As the Fathers of the Second Vatican Council wrote: "Prayer should accompany the reading of Sacred Scripture, so that a dialogue takes place between God and man. For 'we speak to him when we pray; we listen to him when we read the divine oracles'" (*Dogmatic Constitution on Divine Revelation,* 25).

In contemplation we quiet our hearts in Jesus' presence and allow him to touch us, heal us, and move us. Having gone through the door of Scripture, we are now in the chamber of the Lord, our king and friend. In contemplation we gaze upon his beauty and his glory and receive from him the grace and strength to live out the words we have read and meditated upon. Like the two disciples on the road to Emmaus, our hearts can burn with love for God as Jesus opens the Scriptures to us (Luke 24:13-32). God knows exactly what we need, and through contemplation we can stay with him awhile and be encouraged and strengthened by him.

Living in the Word

In Scripture God has set a table of the choicest food for our souls. How can we respond to his invitation to come and eat with him? Very practically, we can plan a specific time of day during which we devote our full attention to his word. We are likely to need to "protect" a set time for reading and prayer. If we wait for some "free time," it may never come along. We also need to choose a private place that is quiet, comfortable, and free from distractions.

How can we prepare our hearts to hear the Lord? Before reading, recall the truths of our faith: God created us out of love; through baptism into Jesus' death and resurrection, we have received forgiveness and freedom; we are all invited to know him personally through the indwelling Holy Spirit; the church is his beloved bride, the gathering of his people; Jesus will return at the end of time to call his people to himself. Establishing these truths at the start can put our minds at rest and give us confidence that God does want to speak to us.

In choosing a daily passage, some people read through a specific book of the Bible, such as Exodus or 1 Corinthians. Others consider a certain biblical theme, such as love, justice, or the kingdom of God. Many follow the liturgical calendar, keeping in touch with the daily Mass readings. Whichever way you choose, open yourself to the Spirit's power to bring the words to life in your heart.

After you've spent time with God's word, it's wise to write out what you've learned. This helps you remember the word and God's lessons. As the truths and character of God are imprinted on our hearts, we increase the great treasure from which we can draw as we face temptations and challenges.

Brothers and sisters, God enjoys sharing his heart with us. He created us to be as intimate with him as children are with their parents, and as a bride is with her husband. Every day, he asks us to spend time with him and receive his word of life. As we open ourselves to his wisdom, we allow him to write his truth on our hearts and to refresh us.

Let us all ask the Spirit to open our minds and hearts to God's word so that we may be more fully conformed to his image.

CHAPTER 5

REVELATION IN THE EUCHARIST

From the very beginning of time, God's intention was that we would all come to him to receive the grace, wisdom, and strength we needed. The Book of Genesis uses the image of the two trees in the garden of Eden to convey this central truth: the tree of life held all the treasures of God's divine plan, and the tree of the knowledge of good and evil represented the philosophy that we could decide for ourselves what was right or wrong—that we didn't need to be fed and sustained by God.

Today, we can encounter the tree of life every time we eat the body of Christ and drink Jesus' blood in Holy Communion. These precious gifts from heaven are meant to sustain us, rejuvenate us, and open us up to the wisdom of God. So in this chapter, we want to take a look at different biblical images that can help us enjoy the presence and power of Jesus at Mass.

Spiritual Food from Heaven

To understand God's desire to fill us with his living bread, we can look back to the Sinai desert, about 1,250 years before Christ. The Israelites had been set free from slavery in Egypt and were headed for the promised land. The journey was hard, food and water scarce.

But here in this lifeless wilderness, God gave his people water from a rock and manna from heaven.

The Bread of the Messiah

More than twelve centuries later, Jesus of Nazareth fed thousands of people with just five loaves of bread and two fish (John 6:1-15). John is quick to point out that this miraculous feeding took place just before the feast of Passover (6:4). John saw this feeding as a prophetic sign linking his readers—and us—to Israel's journey in the desert and at the same time pointing to something far greater: a new Passover, in which God would deliver us not just from physical slavery but from slavery to sin and death.

The Jews of Jesus' day believed that in the coming messianic age the miracle of the manna would be repeated. They believed that this miracle would be performed by the Messiah, the one who would take the place of Moses as Israel's new redeemer (John 6:14; Deuteronomy 18:15). Responding to the people's belief and expanding their hopes even more, Jesus told them that the bread he had come to give would bring eternal life (John 6:32-33). For Jesus, eating this bread—his flesh—was a life-and-death issue, with eternal ramifications.

A Sacrificial Bread

Two prophetic dimensions in this story deserve a closer look: First, Jesus knew that he was going to become an unblemished sacrifice, like the spotless lamb that was sacrificed at every Passover. Second, when he fed the five thousand, Jesus was indicating that the sacrifice of his death on a cross would be manifested to his people in the form of bread. In the prophetic gesture of a miraculous feeding, Jesus linked the image of bread to a spiritual feeding that would become possible because of the sacrifice of his life.

Jesus' words here—"The bread that I will give for the life of the world is my flesh" (John 6:51)—point almost directly to the Last Supper, when he told the twelve: "This is my body, which is given for you" (Luke 22:19). In both instances, he was telling his followers that he was the bread from heaven, God's eternal food that far surpassed the manna in the wilderness.

Those who heard Jesus that day could sense that he was speaking about spiritual life and feeding, not physical life and bread. They could sense that this rabbi who had just fed thousands was speaking about himself as a living sacrifice. Understanding Jesus wasn't their problem. Their problem came in the challenge to accept him and his teaching. It sounded too radical to believe (John 6:52).

Because they could not accept Jesus' words about eating his flesh and drinking his blood, many in the crowd left him (John 6:66). When Jesus saw what was happening, he challenged the apostles to put their faith in him and not walk away. That's when Peter, still wondering why Jesus gave such a hard teaching—and probably wondering if he also should leave—thought, *Where else would I go? Is there anyone else who penetrates my heart the way Jesus does? Is there anyone else who performs such magnificent miracles? Is there anyone else who can give me eternal life? No. He must be the Holy One of God* (see 6:69).

Taste and See

When the apostles were with Jesus, they saw him; they heard him preach; they touched him with their own hands (1 John 1:1-2). Likewise, our senses are the pathways to information. They are like the keyboard of a computer and the microphone of a tape recorder. Through our senses, we receive the information that we can then process in our minds, store in our memories, hold in our hearts.

In the description of the apostles' experience in 1 John, one vital sense was missing: taste. The apostles saw, heard, and touched Jesus. Through their senses, they came to love him, to treasure his words, and to believe that he was the Messiah. But they had not yet grasped what it meant to eat Jesus' flesh as the Bread of Life.

At the Last Supper, when the apostles ate and drank with Jesus, a new dimension was opened up for them, and they were able to internalize their previous experiences with him in a fresh and deeper way. Because eating Jesus' flesh and drinking his blood involves much more than seeing, hearing, and touching the Son of God, they now had a deeper experience of and connection to Jesus—who he was and what he had come to do.

Where Can We Go?

At the Last Supper, God's longing—that we would come to him and be fed by him—was finally fulfilled. Now, at every Mass, Jesus is present to us, inviting us to come and be transformed by eating and drinking his body and blood.

As you receive Jesus this week, try to be like St. Peter. Despite our doubts and areas of resistance to Jesus, in the final analysis, we can echo Peter's proclamation of faith and surrender: "Lord, to whom can we go? You have the words of eternal life. We have come to believe and know that you are the Holy One of God" (John 6:68-69). Trust that when you eat the Bread of Life, Jesus will fulfill his promise and raise you up on the last day (6:54).

Remember: Judas Iscariot was with Peter and Jesus. He ate the same bread as the rest of the twelve, but it did not change him or his mind. So it is clear that the power of the Eucharist to transform us is related, to some degree, to the way we yield ourselves to the gift we are receiving. Notwithstanding a dramatic miracle, the body and blood of Christ will nourish those who are pliable more than it will nourish those who resist its power.

With your whole heart, treasure this spiritual food from heaven every time you receive it. Make sure that you are right with the Lord, and promise that you will be completely open to whatever Jesus wants to say to you and whatever he wants to do in your life. Come to Jesus with a pure and humble heart, and you will find yourself lifted up to God's presence and transformed. This is the way to let the rich food from heaven fill you up and make you whole.

The Grace of Revelation

Every Sunday, millions of people around the world participate in Mass. For some in rural areas, it means traveling long distances. For others with young families, it means dealing with very active children. And for people in some other countries, it even means risking persecution. Still, most congregants don't mind. They will endure whatever they have to because they know that they will receive the Eucharist. It's the Eucharist that draws them, and it's the Eucharist that continues to draw them back again and again.

Let's look at another scriptural image in the hope that it might give us some more insight into the gift of Jesus' body and blood: seeing Jesus through the grace of revelation as we receive him at Mass.

Drawn to Jesus

"Revelation" is the word we use to describe God's work of enlightening our minds and filling our hearts. Like his desire to feed us with his wisdom and grace, God's desire to reveal himself to us stretches back to the very beginning of time.

Near the end of his ministry, Jesus told his disciples, "I, when I am lifted up from the earth, will draw all people to myself" (John 12:32). In one sense, this promise is fulfilled every time we receive the Eucharist. When we eat the Bread of Life, God our Father draws us to his Son. He opens our spiritual eyes and gives us his grace. In fact, the Greek word translated "draw" in this verse also means "drag" or "carry." God is willing to go to extreme lengths to bring us to himself. He will even carry us when we are too weak or too hurt to draw ourselves to him. That's how much he loves us! How does Jesus draw us to himself? With unconditional love, boundless mercy, and heavenly wisdom.

The Moment of Revelation

So often, Jesus is with us but remains hidden. We look, but we cannot see him. We seek him, but we cannot find him. We listen, but we cannot hear him. We are like the two disciples who walked with Jesus on the road to Emmaus but were kept from recognizing him (Luke 24:13-35). These disciples were having doubts about Jesus, and he engaged them in conversation to try to help them. Beginning with Moses, he used Scripture to explain how everything that was written about the Christ would come true—and their hearts began to burn again. Jesus was drawing these two disciples to him. Like the apostles, they saw Jesus, they touched him and heard him; their hearts were even burning for God. But their eyes were opened to recognize Jesus only when Jesus blessed the bread and broke it.

Jesus wants to teach us. Through the Holy Spirit, he wants to take everything he taught his apostles and give it to us as well. He wants to reveal God's wisdom to us so that we can have "the mind of Christ" (1 Corinthians 2:16). As amazing as Jesus' revelation in the Emmaus story, *our* eyes can be opened just as powerfully as ordinary bread is transformed into the body of Christ at every Mass.

Compelled to Work for God

It was nightfall. Even though these two disciples were tired, they did not go home to rest after Jesus revealed himself to them. Instead, they returned immediately to Jerusalem to tell Peter and the others about how they had recognized the Lord when they broke bread together (Luke 24:33-35). This final detail illustrates a great work of the Eucharist: It compels us to serve Jesus. These two disciples were so full of joy that they had to share what they had experienced. Likewise, when we see Jesus for who he is, we too will feel compelled to serve him.

On another occasion—also after Easter Sunday—some of the apostles were coming in from a fruitless fishing expedition (John 21:1-19). They saw Jesus on the shore but didn't recognize him. He told them to cast their nets once more. When they did, they caught so many fish that their nets were straining. Only then did one of them recognize Jesus.

When they came ashore, Jesus broke some bread and gave it to them for breakfast. In this little gesture, Jesus was telling the apostles, "Know that I am with you, ready to help you and ready to feed you as you feed my sheep." This story further illustrates a simple pattern in Scripture: when we take and receive what Jesus gives to us, we are compelled to go out and give it to others. Jesus wants us to collect everyone—the poor and the rich, the educated and the uneducated, the young and the old. He wants us to bring them all to him, confident that he is with us, guiding us and empowering us, even until the end of time (Matthew 28:19-20).

Be Alert

Let's suppose that the two disciples on the road to Emmaus had invited Jesus to walk with them but had lost interest as he explained Scripture. Maybe one was eager to get home and the other was preoccupied with other obligations. What would have happened? The event probably wouldn't have been recorded in Scripture, because nothing special would have occurred. But something incredible did happen, because the disciples were attentive to what this "stranger" had to say.

Brothers and sisters, without careful listening, we will not see God. We will not recognize him—even after we eat the Bread of Life. And if we don't hear the Lord's revelation, how are we going to know when and where to cast our nets? When we are distracted, we limit what Jesus wants to do through us because we haven't been attentive to the way his body and blood can transform us.

But this didn't happen to the disciples on the road, nor to the apostles in the boat. They were attentive, they listened, and they obeyed. Jesus wants to do this same work in us. He wants both to reveal himself to us, and to see us give away to others everything that he has given to us.

A Covenant of Love

In addition to revealing Jesus to us and compelling us to work for him, the Eucharist also reveals God's eternal covenant with us. Every time we receive Jesus' body and blood, we can hear him telling us again and again: "I will be your God, and you will be my people."

Throughout Scripture, in the stories of Adam and Eve, Noah, Abraham, Moses, and David, we see how God has always wanted to have an intimate, covenant relationship with us. This desire is present in all of the prophets; it is a central theme in the gospels; it is explained in the letters; and it reaches its dramatic climax in the Book of Revelation. In fact, God's love for us expressed through his covenant is one of the most beautiful images in all of Scripture, and it is the very foundation of the mysteries we celebrate at Mass.

The God of the Covenant

The crux of our covenant with God involves responsibilities on both sides. On God's side, he promises to be our God—to give us his Spirit, to reveal himself to us, to put his laws in our hearts, to forgive us, and to care for our welfare. On our side, God asks us to be his people—to love him, to be faithful to him, to turn to him for help, to refuse any form of idol worship, and to obey his commands.

Throughout history, God has always upheld his side of the covenant, while we have not been so faithful. Our love for him has been erratic. We haven't always obeyed his commands. We have worshipped idols. Again and again, we have sold our birthright. But instead of turning from us and rejecting us, our heavenly Father continues to reach out in the hope of drawing us home.

Think about the story of Hosea and his wife, Gomer (Hosea 1–3). Gomer caused Hosea great heartache because of her unfaithfulness; but despite all the pain, Hosea learned two important messages, which he passed on to the people of Israel. The first message was that Israel had treated God just as Gomer had treated Hosea. And second, through his faithfulness to Gomer, Hosea learned that

God would continue to love unfaithful Israel and try to bring her back to himself. In a way, this is a microcosm of the story of God's covenant love for us.

Though much of the history of God's dealings with Israel was marked by the people's unfaithfulness, God finally sent his Son to fulfill the covenant in every way. Not once did Jesus turn away from his Father. Not once did he sin. And when Jesus broke the bread and blessed the wine at the Last Supper, this Son of David became the new covenant between God and humanity. By his own blood, he ratified a new covenant with God for all of us.

This new covenant is what we celebrate every time we celebrate the Mass. By gathering around the table of the Lord, we embrace God's new covenant with us and pledge to uphold our side. At the same time, the Mass is God's greatest opportunity to write this covenant on our hearts and convince us that he will never abandon us.

The New Covenant: An Event and a Sacrament

As mysterious as it may sound, the new covenant that we celebrate at Mass is both a historical event that took place on the cross and a sacrament of grace that transcends time and place. It is true that the sacrifice of Jesus will never be repeated. It happened once, for all time (Hebrews 10:14). Yet Jesus told us to relive this sacrifice every time we celebrate the Eucharist (1 Corinthians 11:24). Like Mary, we may want to ask, "How can this be?" (Luke 1:34). Perhaps the words of one of the Fathers of the Church, St. John of Damascus, can help us here:

You ask, how can the bread become the Body of Christ
and the wine . . . the Blood of Christ. I shall tell you: the
Holy Spirit comes upon them and accomplishes what
surpasses every word and thought. . . . Let it be enough
for you to understand that it is by the Holy Spirit that the
Lord, through and in himself, took flesh. (*An Exposition
of the Orthodox Faith,* 4.13)

We may never understand the mystery of the Eucharist. But
neither should we let that stop us from receiving its blessings.
Perhaps it is enough for us to know that Jesus has told us to do this
in memory of him. Perhaps it is enough to believe that eating and
drinking of the Lord can have a life-changing impact upon us.

Protected by the Eucharist

One popular diet these days is called the "catabolic diet." It champions
foods that help you burn more calories than you take in: carrots, cel-
ery, asparagus, and the like. The catabolic diet promises that as you eat
you can actually lose weight. Although the analogy is not perfect, we
might see some similarities here with the Eucharist. When we receive
the body and blood of Christ, we receive the power to fight against sin.
The more we partake of the Eucharist, the more our tendencies to sin
are eaten up. In other words, when we eat the Bread of Life, we lose
"sin-weight"!

When Jesus said, "this is my blood of the covenant, which is
poured out for many for the forgiveness of sins" (Matthew 26:28),

he was saying that his blood offering contained an element of protection. Back in Egypt, when God told Moses how to prepare for the angel of death, he told the people to take some of the blood from their Passover sacrifice and put it "on the two doorposts and the lintel" of their homes. "When I see the blood," God promised, "I will pass over you, and no plague shall destroy you" (Exodus 12:7, 13).

If God used the blood of a lamb to protect the Israelites who partook of that same lamb, will he not protect us from the ravages of sin when we eat the flesh and drink the blood of Jesus, the Lamb of God? Every time we eat and drink, we are not just renewing a legal covenant; we are entering into the strong, loving arms of God. We belong to him, and he will protect us and keep us as we stay close to him.

Pray for Renewal

A chapter on the Eucharist would be incomplete if we did not ask one more question: Given all that the Eucharist does for us and all that is ours in the new covenant, why isn't the church perfect? Why is there so much division? Why is there so much selfishness and disobedience? Why is there so much complacency?

Although any answers would be long and complex, one thing is clear: unity in the church is integrally linked with an ever-deepening appreciation of the Eucharist. Every piece of bread that we eat is made up of thousands of granules of wheat. Every cup of wine that we drink is a mixture of thousands of grapes. Yet when we eat

Jesus' body and drink his blood, we are all eating one Eucharist. We are all participating in one eternal covenant.

Just as Jesus and his Father are one, God wants us to be one—not separated by division, disobedience, or indifference—but bound together in a covenant of love and faithfulness. The Eucharist has divine power to take us to a deeper level of unity. It makes us, the individual members of the church, like grains of wheat in a single loaf of bread or grapes crushed into one cup. Communion heightens communion. It kneads us and crushes us and makes us into the one, holy, catholic, and apostolic church that our Father so desires.

Let us ask the Holy Spirit to awaken in us a spirit of unity and love. May God continue to bless us and our whole church as we partake of the Bread of Life.

CHAPTER 6

COME TO GOD'S HOUSE: MEETING JESUS AT MASS

As a young couple, Bob and Kathy McCarthy wanted to teach their children the importance of being a family. So they set aside Sunday as a special day to spend together. After church, they would play games and have fun as a family. The day was always capped with a special dinner.

Even after their children had grown and begun their own families, the whole McCarthy clan continued to gather every Sunday. Everyone looked forward to the feast. Grandpa especially loved holding his youngest grandchild and marveling at the family resemblance. The adult children enjoyed being with their parents. They didn't come home because their presence was expected. They came because they loved their parents and appreciated everything their parents had done for them.

This analogy can give us a glimpse of what Sunday Mass can become for us. Every week our heavenly Father invites us to his house so that we can spend time with him and gather around his table as one family.

In this chapter, we want to examine our disposition and attitudes as we come to Mass. Are we prepared to receive everything that God has in store for us? And then we'll discuss segments of the Mass to understand how various parts—the penitential rite, the Scripture readings, the intercessions, the Eucharistic prayer, and communion—are intended to draw us closer to God's throne of grace.

Invited to the Banquet

Jesus Wants More than Our Attendance

At every Mass, we have two choices: we can "go through the motions," reciting the prayers but remaining distant from God. Or we can have a life-changing encounter with the living God. Jesus wants so much more than our attendance. Like a bridegroom gazing at his bride, he longs for intimacy with his people. Every gathering at Mass is a precursor to the marriage feast of the Lamb, when Jesus will return to gather the church to himself and present her, holy and blameless, to his Father. As his beloved bride, we belong to Jesus, and it's at Mass that we come together to receive his love.

This is what God wants our experience of liturgy to be every day. During worship, when our hearts are open to receiving life from the Spirit, he wants us to experience the fulfillment of one of the central promises of Scripture: "God is love, and he who abides in love abides in God, and God abides in him" (1 John 4:16).

Grace Limited Only by Our Attitudes

Have you ever noticed that the liturgy contains all of the major components of prayer? Think about it: at every Mass, we repent of our sins; we hear God's voice; we proclaim who he is in the creed; we intercede with the power and authority of children of God; we meet Jesus personally at the Eucharistic feast; and we worship him and give him thanks. When our hearts and minds are set on the risen Christ, Mass can become a time of deep adoration and praise, a time of intimate communion with the One who created us and has redeemed us.

This is why we need to stay alert and expectant during Mass. Distracting attitudes—from boredom to anxiety to frustration with the demands of life—can keep us from encountering God deeply. Tiredness and passivity also can rob us of our experience of the presence of God.

But it isn't just a human battle that we have to fight. We are also engaged in a spiritual battle during Mass. Satan is constantly trying to disrupt us by introducing little doubts into our minds about whether it is even possible to experience God and hear his voice. He urges us away from prayer, worship, and unity with the people around us. He knows that if he can convince us to isolate ourselves, we will miss out on the blessings God has reserved for us. The evil one hates worship of God, and he will take advantage of our minds' reluctance to enter into the presence of God.

In contrast, God delights in the presence and attention of his children. Like a loving Father, he teaches us, forms us in his wisdom, and pours out his love upon us.

Examining Your Heart before Mass

If possible, try to get to church a few minutes before Mass starts to prepare your heart for all that God intends to give you during the liturgy. Take some time to ponder the following questions and to settle your heart in God's presence.

1. Can I look upon the Mass as a lavish banquet that God has prepared for me and for everyone else in this church?

2. What thoughts or attitudes might try to keep me from lifting up my heart to God during Mass? Can I recognize the spiritual battle in which the evil one wants to rob me of my sense of God's presence?

3. Am I ready—to the best of my ability—to worship the Lord with my whole heart during Mass?

4. Can I see the people around me as part of God's family?

Meeting Jesus at Mass

Every one of us has a special calling that God prepared for us before the beginning of creation. "He chose us in Christ before the foundation of the world, that we should be holy and blameless before him in love" (Ephesians 1:4). He has given each of us special gifts and called us to use them to build his kingdom. But beyond our individual callings, God has called us together as the body of Christ to worship him in love and unity. At Mass, he calls us together and empowers us to be good stewards of our gifts. Consider the many blessings that have been received in the context of the Mass. The early church experienced the Eucharist as a time when members of the body of Christ prayed together for the whole church, for her people, and for her mission. When the first Christians gathered for the *agapé* meal, they came together for fellowship, to receive teaching, to pray together, and to celebrate "the breaking of bread" (Acts 2:42).

Let's mine some of the treasures that are available in the liturgy for those who come to the altar with open hearts. In each section of the Mass—from the Penitential Rite and the Liturgy of the Word through the eucharistic prayer and Communion—Jesus eagerly awaits us, ready to reveal heavenly mysteries.

"I Confess . . . "

Early in the liturgy, we repent for our sins, and with the humility of a servant, Jesus cleanses us. He removes the chains of guilt and enables us to enter God's presence. Try to visualize Jesus as he washed the feet of his disciples (see John 13:1-11). He told them that they did not need to have their whole bodies washed, only their feet. Similarly, unless we have committed a mortal sin, we do not need the complete bath we received in baptism—but we *do* need to be washed clean of the venial sins of self-love that dirty our feet each day. Whether through judgmental thoughts of the mind or angry outbursts of our tongues, we all sin. And yet these transgressions do not wipe out the miracle of forgiveness that we received in baptism.

Satan will do anything to keep us from repentance. In his attempts to minimize sin, he will whisper to us, "Don't worry about that little thing; you have a right to be angry or jealous or greedy." But however big or small it is, our sin saddens God, because it hinders the intimacy that he wants to have with us.

So as you come to Mass, be courageous. Face your sin and repent of it. Come to your Father and ask his forgiveness. Repent of any dispositions that prevent you from having a close friendship with him. Tell him that you are sorry for any anger, fears, lustful thoughts or actions, or even apathy toward God. As you do, you will find freedom to enter the throne room of God.

The Living Word

The writer of the Letter to the Hebrews tells us that God's word is "living and active, sharper than any two-edged sword . . . discerning the thoughts and intentions of the heart" (Hebrews 4:12). God wants to cut us away from all that is false and fill us with the truth instead. When we are eager and attentive, the Spirit of God can speak to us in the Scripture readings and reveal God's mind to us.

"Hearing" God's word can be quite different from "listening" to it. Hearing is limited to our ears receiving sound waves and sending signals to the brain for interpretation. But listening requires that we pay close attention. We may sometimes think, *I listen, but how can I hear God speaking?* This is why we have to trust that when we quiet our hearts and listen to his word, God will surely speak words of comfort, correction, and peace to us.

Lack of contact with Scripture can cause us to grow cold toward God. Conversely, when we allow his word to penetrate our hearts, we will hear the Spirit speaking gently to us. When we are convinced that the Scriptures are "truth" rather than just another opinion and that they are God's voice rather than just his dictates, confusion will give way to clarity; our actions will flow from God's word rather than from our feelings.

Intercession

Jesus encouraged his disciples to pray together and to expect prayers to be powerfully answered for the whole church, for "where two or three are gathered in my name, there am I in the midst of them" (Matthew 18:20). When we consider the millions of baptized faithful praying together on Sundays, it is evident that our prayers offered together have the potential to extend throughout the church. Each believer receives grace and blessing from the prayer and worship of the whole church.

"I Am the Bread of Life"

Receiving the body and blood of Christ is not something that we simply "do." In the Liturgy of the Eucharist we can come face-to-face, heart-to-heart, with Jesus. By exercising our faith, we can encounter Jesus in the consecrated bread and wine. When we are content with our own reason, we risk missing the wonder and intimacy of this encounter.

The early church faced the same challenge we face today. Both St. Paul and St. John warned their followers to have the right heart in their celebrations of the Eucharist. When the Corinthians took the Communion table lightly, Paul wrote sternly that whoever "eats the bread or drinks the cup of the Lord in an unworthy manner will be guilty of profaning the body and blood of the Lord" (1 Corinthians 11:27). It's great that millions receive the body of Christ each week. And yet Paul's words still confront us all: do we come to the table worthily, with a deep desire to receive life from Jesus?

In his teaching on the Eucharist, St. John wrote of a growing tension between Jesus and many of his followers (John 6). They tried to make Jesus' words fit into the categories of human reason, but Jesus was trying to raise them up with the logic of divine love: "Do not labor for the food which perishes, but for the food which endures to eternal life, which the Son of man will give to you" (6:27).

The people's response showed that they were placing their confidence in themselves more than in the grace of God: "What must we do, to be doing the works of God?" (John 6:28). But Jesus continued to urge them (and us) to rely on the truth and trust in God:

"Just believe in me. Stay close to me, rely on me, abide in me" (see 6:29). Jesus is always seeking to raise his followers up to heaven. Every time we approach the altar, we should recall Jesus' promise: "I am the bread of life; he who comes to me shall not hunger, and he who believes in me shall never thirst" (6:35).

Communion and the Cross of Christ

As he gathered with his apostles in the upper room, Jesus knew that his "time" was drawing near. And so he transformed their final Passover meal together into a feast of love with his closest friends. Today the Eucharist remains that same feast of love between Jesus and all of us, whom he delights to call his friends (John 15:15).

At the Last Supper, Jesus told the apostles, "Do this in remembrance of me" (Luke 22:19). May we never forget that Jesus is our bread. He is our life, our hope, and our truth. As we partake of the Bread of Life, Jesus wants to raise our minds to heaven. He wants us to imagine ourselves at the heavenly banquet, seated at table with him and all his people. When we come face-to-face with the Lord in the presence of all the angels and saints, how can we help but worship him and thank him for everything that he has done for us?

After you have received Jesus' body and blood, spend a few minutes gazing at the cross in the sanctuary. Contemplate the beautiful fact that you can receive Jesus in this marvelous way only because he shed his blood for you—he died in your place—at Calvary. *We* were the guilty ones, but *he* took upon himself our guilt and shame. What pain must have consumed the Father's heart as he watched his only Son die a criminal's death! And yet, how his heart must have been filled with love for humanity and all creation. It is finally accomplished! In the death and resurrection of Jesus, the mystery of God's love has conquered sin. In the cross, we see both incredible beauty and unimaginable suffering. We can see the love and healing that Jesus offers us every time we receive his body and blood.

What more can we say about the treasures of the liturgy? Jesus offers so much more than we could ever express. How moving it is when God's children cry out, "Our Father!" How pleasing it is when they offer each other the kiss of peace. We could spend hours dwelling on the truths proclaimed in the creed. Our hope is that every time you attend Mass, you will be satisfied with nothing less than meeting Jesus, worshipping him, and receiving his grace.

CHAPTER 7

FINDING FREEDOM THROUGH FORGIVENESS AND REPENTANCE

When five-year-old boys get in a fight, they seem to be able to get past their differences quickly. But for adults, repentance and forgiveness seem much more difficult. Perhaps it's because we can tell the difference between saying or hearing a cursory "I'm sorry" and humbly asking someone—or being asked—for forgiveness.

We can become more forgiving persons only as we come to see how much we have been forgiven by God. As we become more sensitive to the sins and defects in our own lives and turn to the Lord in repentance, we find not only that he is eager to give us his mercy, but that repentance itself leads to a new grace that can transform us. We find that forgiveness not only leads us closer to God; it also leads us closer to our brothers and sisters in Christ. The Sacrament of Reconciliation offers us the opportunity and the grace to be reconciled at all times with God and with one another. Taking our faith personally means that we say often, both to God and to those close to us, "I'm sorry. Please forgive me." It also means that when we are asked for forgiveness, we readily forgive. How different our world would be if every Christian practiced this essential element of our faith!

In this chapter we'll look at three facets of the freedom and healing available through forgiveness and repentance—as we forgive others for wounding us and as we repent of our own sins and also for those of the church.

Forgiving Those Who Have Wounded Us

The Quality of Mercy

When someone has wounded us deeply, sometimes we can't find it within ourselves to forgive. In such situations, we might hear the adage, "Time heals all wounds." There is some truth to this, but time can do only so much, and the healing may be only partial. Or we may be told to "forgive and forget." But few of us can erase our memories as we would a chalkboard. And even if we could forget, simply walking away from past hurts won't get us to the point where our wounds are replaced by peace, or where we are able to bless the person who has hurt us. No, the answer must lie somewhere else.

If we look at the challenge of forgiveness through the teachings of the gospel, we find a new perspective: when forgiveness seems impossible, it's usually a sign that we need to return to God and ponder his mercy more deeply. That's the only way we'll be able to rise above the limitations of our fallen nature and be filled with the divine power we need.

Imagine how deep God's mercy runs. From the beginning of time, God has loved every single person unconditionally. Yet, despite God's constancy and faithfulness, humanity has ignored him, bypassed him, and even sinned against him directly. And still,

God continues to love. He never turns away. As St. Paul wrote, "While we still were sinners Christ died for us" (Romans 5:8). That's the nature of divine mercy. At Calvary, Jesus and the Father cried out to all of us, "Your sins are forgiven!"

Redeeming the Past

God's mercy is so deep and powerful that the cross has not only removed our sins, it has also empowered us to forgive as completely as we have been forgiven. Jesus doesn't want us to forget the past. He wants to *redeem* our past as we learn to echo his words from the cross: "Father, forgive them."

Scripture says that Jesus ransomed us from the futile ways of our ancestors (1 Peter 1:18). No longer bound by the "futile ways" of our life of sin, we can look upon our past with new eyes—the eyes of God. We can see how he has always been with us, blessing us even when we didn't recognize him. Released from our futile ways of thinking and acting, we can look upon everything through the lenses of mercy, love, and gratitude rather than regret, judgment, and reproach.

No longer under the shadow of our past, we can also begin to look upon those who have hurt us with the same kind of mercy God has toward us. The lenses of blame, hatred, and bitterness will be lifted. And this new compassionate vision will move us to forgive.

"Forgive as I Have Forgiven You"

Jesus' command to forgive "seventy times seven" times (Matthew 18:22) reflects God's unlimited forgiveness for us. Having poured his love into our hearts, he now expects us to forgive others just as unconditionally. Jesus never said, "Wait until they ask for forgiveness." He simply said, "Forgive as I have forgiven you." Jesus taught this lesson—as hard as it may seem—so that we could understand that withholding forgiveness benefits nobody. In fact, holding on to our past hurts gets in the way of our relationship with Jesus and diminishes our experience of being God's beloved children.

Jesus taught his disciples that their willingness to forgive is linked to God's forgiveness of their own sins. In the parable of the unmerciful servant (Matthew 18:21-35), Jesus said that because the servant was unwilling to forgive a trivial debt, his master refused to forgive his immense debt. Does this mean that God holds back his mercy and his forgiveness? No. It means that when we fail to forgive, we cloud our relationship with God and cut ourselves off from the his mercy. Jesus has already died for our sins. His compassion and mercy are always flowing. But we must forgive so that the channel of his grace is open to us.

Forgiveness brings freedom. When we forgive other people, even in a limited or imperfect way, we open the door for God's grace to release us from a prison of resentment and pain. Our God is a God of peace. He wants us to live in his peace, not just for our own sake, but for the sake of those around us. God wants us to be free from our hurts so that we can spend our energy loving our families and friends, serving the needy, and giving of ourselves in the church.

Freedom Today

So what can we do today? Pray a prayer of forgiveness right now for one person who has hurt you. If you find yourself unable to pray for someone who has hurt you deeply, choose instead someone whose offense was less painful. Do your best and know that Jesus will abundantly bless your effort.

"Dear Jesus, you gave every ounce of your life so that I could know your unconditional love. Let that love flow into me now so that I can forgive (name) with all my heart. I may not feel like forgiving him or her at this moment, but that doesn't matter. As you have forgiven my many sins, so I forgive (name). I do not hold (name) bound; I release him or her completely. And I don't need (name) to reciprocate. I offer forgiveness without expecting anything in return, just as you did. Bless (name), Lord. I totally rely on your power in praying this prayer. Amen."

Repenting of My Sins

True repentance involves a genuine sorrow for the hurt we have caused and an intention to change. How intimidating this can seem! No wonder we find it difficult! But if we look closely at Scripture, we can recognize another, more freeing, truth: first and foremost, repentance is the work of the Holy Spirit to soften our hearts and make us like Jesus.

The Spirit's Work in Repentance

We can never hear it enough: one of the greatest gifts God gives us is the Holy Spirit. Through the Spirit, our hearts can be lifted up to heaven. Through the Spirit, we receive the power to live as Jesus did. And through the Spirit, we learn to repent of our sins and receive God's purifying love.

In Scripture, King David is often linked with repentance. Although the story of David's sin with Bathsheba and its aftermath says very little about David's repentance (2 Samuel 11–12), Psalm 51 gives a detailed picture of what may have been going through David's mind as he considered the consequences of his actions and brought his sin before God for forgiveness. Let's look at this psalm to get a glimpse into the heart of true repentance.

Have Mercy, Lord!

As he faced up to the sins he had committed and the inner drives that had led him to sin, David cried out, "Create in me a clean heart, O God, and put a new and right spirit within me" (Psalm 51:10). David realized that he couldn't change his heart on his own. The best he could do was to try to hide or run away from his lusts. Only God could make him into a new creation. Only God could free him from the desires that had caused so much havoc. It wasn't enough simply to apologize. David needed to be changed deep in his heart.

David also understood that there was more to his sin than its devastating effect on Bathsheba, Uriah, and the people of Israel: "Against you, you alone, have I sinned, and done what is evil in your sight" (Psalm 51:4). At the heart of his sin was the sorrow it brought to God. How often do we consider the way our sin affects our relationship with God? When we sin, we erect a barrier between ourselves and our loving Father. We tell him that he isn't welcome in our hearts. Ultimately, sin can even cut off the flow of God's grace and protection over our lives. No wonder all of heaven rejoices every time one of us repents and welcomes Jesus back into his or her heart (Luke 15:7)!

When we recognize and acknowledge our sins, we can be sure that the Holy Spirit is at work in us. Every day, God invites us to examine our thoughts and deeds and ask his Spirit to uncover our sin. It's not because he wants to make us feel guilty, but because he wants us to receive his healing and purification. As David acknowledged, only God can remove guilt and shame (Psalm 51:2), convince us not to sin again (51:12), and make us into more loving, compassionate people (51:13).

Freedom from Feelings of Guilt

Have you ever felt guilty, even after receiving the Sacrament of Reconciliation or after having apologized to a friend? You know that you've been forgiven, but your conscience still bothers you.

You know that God doesn't want to see you bound in guilt and shame, but you can't seem to shake the feeling. How do you get free?

The first step is to recognize God's healing power whenever you ask forgiveness or receive absolution. Accept by faith that God has forgiven you and wants to heal you. Stand against feelings of guilt! Don't let them rule your conscience. Believe that healing has occurred, even if you don't feel it.

If your mind continues to dredge up memories of past sin, ask the Holy Spirit to rein in your thoughts. It's amazing how our memories can replay the same scenes, like a tape recorder, and leave us gripped by guilt. As soon as shame over past financial debt, guilt over sexual temptation or sin, or remorse over envious thoughts or bitter words spring up, turn to the Lord: "Holy Spirit, I know that you dwell in me. I submit my thoughts and memories to you. Come and set me free!"

Finally, acknowledge that God's love for you is greater than any sin you could ever commit. State in your heart that God wants to set you free because he loves you too much to keep you in darkness.

Remorse or Repentance?

A great example of the difference between the shame that comes with remorse and the freedom that comes with repentance happened the day Jesus was crucified. Both Judas and Peter had rejected the Lord (Luke 22:47-62), but they illustrate radically different reactions to sin.

Judas was so overcome by guilt that he hanged himself (Matthew 27:3-5). Judas was so badgered by the memory of his betrayal that he seems to have forgotten everything he learned as a disciple of Jesus. He lost sight of how much Jesus loved him and how much Jesus had already healed and forgiven him. All he could see was his sin, and it drained him of hope. Convinced he could never be forgiven, in despair he ended his life.

Peter was also shaken to the core after he denied knowing Jesus (Matthew 26:75). Under pressure, this "rock" of the church realized that Jesus wasn't his primary concern at all. Self-preservation won out. But Peter's sorrow was different from Judas'. Despite the bitter memory of his denial, Peter recalled Jesus' promises of forgiveness; he brought his sin before God and asked for pardon and peace. As a result, Peter became a more humble and compassionate man of God.

This is how the Spirit works. He convicts us of sin; at the same time he fills us with hope that we can be forgiven and changed.

Our sins are not God's primary concern. Loving him, honoring him, and yielding our wills to him—these are the true desires of his heart. Our God wants to make us as pure and spotless as a bride on her wedding day. And to accomplish this, he sends us his Spirit to lead us on the path of repentance (Ephesians 5:25-27).

Brothers and sisters, never lose hope! You can draw close to God at any moment. His Spirit is always moving you to repentance, always ready to reveal how much Jesus loves you. Every day, the Holy Spirit wants to confront your self-sufficiency and weakness so that you can be set free to experience God's presence.

Seven Simple Steps toward Repentance

1. Every evening or morning, review the previous day. Begin by quieting your mind so that you can hear the Holy Spirit speaking to your conscience.

2. Ask the Spirit to show you any wrongdoing—in your thoughts and desires, in your words and relationships, and in your actions.

3. Think about how the sins you see have clouded your experience of and trust in the Lord's love.

4. Check your heart: Are you pliable and willing to change your mind about these sins? Do you feel unwilling to change? Do you have any sense that it's hopeless even to try?

5. Cling to God. Acknowledge that he is your strength, and tell him that you want him to reform your mind so that you will think as he wants you to think and choose as he wants you to choose. Renounce any drive in you that wants to remain independent of the Lord.

6. Place yourself in God's hands and obey whatever you think he is asking you to do. As you practice, God's voice will become clearer.

7. Move from thought to action. Take one or two concrete
steps to overcome or avoid that sin area the next day.
Remember: Jesus is with you every step of the way!

Repenting of the Sins of God's People

The gifts of repentance and forgiveness can take us beyond our
own individual concerns. They can teach us to see the people of
God with new eyes. These lessons were most clearly illustrated
by the late Pope John Paul II. He was the first pope ever to visit
the Jewish synagogue in Rome. He spoke out boldly on behalf of
people suffering political and economic oppression. He traveled
the globe many times, proclaiming Christ to millions. He reached
out to Christians of all traditions, seeking to build the unity that has
eluded us for centuries.

History may record one event as the most all-encompassing
image of his pontificate: During Mass in St. Peter's Basilica, on
the first Sunday of Lent in the Jubilee Year 2000, he asked God's
forgiveness for the sins of the people of God over the past thousand
years. Never in history had a pope taken such a bold step!

Just as John Paul II was moved by the Holy Spirit to repent for
the sins of the past, we, the people of God, are called to follow
his example. We too need to ask the Spirit to show us our need to
repent, not just for our own sins, but for the sins of the people of
God as a whole. God promises, "If my people who are called by my
name humble themselves, pray, seek my face, and turn from their

wicked ways, then I will hear from heaven, and will forgive their sin and heal their land" (2 Chronicles 7:14).

In offering these prayers of repentance, the Holy Father was following the example of many people in Scripture who experienced a similar urging of the Spirit. The Old Testament gives several beautiful examples, including the layman Nehemiah and the priest Ezra, whose stories center on the destruction of Jerusalem by the Babylonian army and its aftermath.

Nehemiah: These Are My People

About 450 years before Christ, Nehemiah, a faithful Jew in the court of the king of Persia, learned about the miserable conditions of the Jews living in Jerusalem. Jerusalem had been invaded by Nebuchadnezzar of Babylon; its walls had been torn down; its temple—the dwelling place of Yahweh—had been burnt to the ground. Most of the people had been deported to Babylon; only the poorest had been left behind with next to nothing to sustain them.

When news of his people's suffering reached him, Nehemiah wept for days, "fasting and praying before the God of heaven" (Nehemiah 1:4). Humbly confessing the sins of his people, he reminded God of his covenant love for the Hebrew children—a covenant that could never be broken. Nehemiah knew that, being one of God's chosen people, he was somehow linked with every child of Israel. He shared responsibility for the state of their nation.

The struggles of the Jews so pierced Nehemiah's heart that he left the security of the Persian court and returned to Jerusalem.

Once there, he devoted himself to encouraging the people and helping them rebuild the city walls. Imagine the risks Nehemiah took. Imagine the sacrifices he made. Because he was moved to pray and repent, his life would never be the same.

Ezra: Rebuilding the People's Hearts

Ezra, a Jewish priest living in Jerusalem a short time before Nehemiah arrived, was similarly appalled at the condition of God's people; he mourned the fact that they had lost their sense of being God's chosen, special possession and the fact that they had lost their conviction that only Yahweh was worthy of their worship. They could see no difference between themselves and the pagans living just outside the holy city.

Ezra's story shows us a priest suffering greatly over the condition of God's people: "From the days of our ancestors to this day we have been deep in guilt. . . . We are slaves, yet our God has not forsaken us in our slavery, but has extended to us his steadfast love" (Ezra 9:7, 9). Spurred on by his trust in Yahweh's love for his people, Ezra set out to rebuild the temple. But later he realized that the physical building wouldn't be enough. Knowing that the people's vision of themselves and their sense of God's love needed to be rebuilt, he dedicated himself to restoring the covenant as the heart of the people's life together.

Taken together, Ezra and Nehemiah show that all of us—lay, priest, and religious—are called to repent for our sins and for the sins of all believers. It's not up to the Holy Father alone. He has set the example, but we all must join him in begging God to forgive and heal.

A Sense of Family

One element unites Pope John Paul II with these Old Testament figures: a clear sense of unity with all the people of God. Buildings, organizations, committees—none of these make up the heart of the church. The church is all about Jesus' desire to draw his people together as one body. With all God's people, we are one family, not just individuals living isolated lives.

When we understand that we are part of this body, we recognize that we are no different from anyone else. St. Paul could call himself "the foremost" of sinners (1 Timothy 1:15) because he knew that he was as much in need of forgiveness as anyone else. In our day, when the Holy Father repents for the sins of the past thousand years, each of us needs to realize that, but for God's grace in our lives, we are just as capable of committing the same sins as our predecessors.

Race, education, and social status do not separate God's people. We are all one in baptism (1 Corinthians 12:13). The inmate in prison is no less vital than the most influential bishop; we all are members of one body.

One with the Body Today

Many of us love to recall the lives of the saints. Reading about them makes us feel close to heroes of another age and in unity with the body of Christ. But it's just as important that we join our hearts with every brother and sister alive today. We are intimately connected with the whole family of God—the greatest of saints and the worst of sinners. The more we understand this truth, the more we will be compelled to get on our knees and repent for the sins, even the crimes that have been committed by our brothers and sisters.

When Pope John Paul II visited Israel in 2000, he indicated that his repentance to the Lord and to the Jewish people was not about political gain or improving his image. His only desire was to seek a healing of memories that would bring all God's people closer together. While most of us are not called to speak publicly on such matters, we are all called to have the same heart, asking God to forgive all the times that Christians have been poor witnesses to Jesus and his church.

Father, Forgive!

How many of us have suffered over broken marriages and families—either our own or of someone we love. In much the same way, our heavenly Father weeps over his children when they are bound in sin or divided from each other. How pleased he is when we wash one another's feet on Holy Thursday as a gesture of unity and humility—and with heartfelt repentance and forgiveness.

If the Holy Father, at the turn of the millennium, could repent on such a large scale, can we play our part and repent on a small scale? Who knows what grace will flow from the throne of God as a result of our prayer? Let's hold onto this precious promise from the Lord: "If my people who are called by my name humble themselves, pray, seek my face, and turn from their wicked ways, then I will hear from heaven, and will forgive their sin and heal their land" (2 Chronicles 7:14).

CHAPTER 8

COMING TO KNOW
THE HOLY SPIRIT

In the early 1900s, millions of Europeans came to America looking for new opportunities. In wave after wave, they came by boat, eager to join the rapidly expanding workforce of a growing country. Many who made the journey, however, didn't understand the terms of their transport. Wanting to save money, these immigrants brought their own food on board the ship. While other passengers enjoyed the rich fare in the ships' dining halls, these families stayed in their cabins, rationing cold meats and dried fruits and hoping for the best. They didn't know that the price of their tickets included three meals a day!

This story is a good analogy for our Christian lives. As believers baptized into Christ, we have received the Holy Spirit. God himself lives in our hearts—and not just passively. He wants to impart to us everything Jesus taught and everything he won on the cross. He wants to give us "every spiritual blessing in the heavenly places" (Ephesians 1:3) and become the guiding force in our lives. Such a rich banquet of divine grace is included in our "baptismal ticket," but so often we settle for cold meats and dried fruit!

For many believers, the Holy Spirit remains a relatively unknown member of the Trinity, and this makes it very difficult to experience everything God has planned for us. So let's look at who the Holy

Spirit is and what he does so we can better understand how we can experience the Spirit and his power more deeply.

Coming to Know "God the Forgotten"

As Christians, we are familiar with our heavenly Father. We recognize him as God. We describe him as holy, all-knowing, all-powerful, merciful, forgiving, and loving. When we meditate on him, we see a loving Father who gave us life, who intimately cares for us, and who wants to share himself with us. Although we sense that these descriptions are inadequate, we also know that they can go a long way in helping us reach out to him.

We can say similar things about Jesus. As the Son of God, the Second Person of the Trinity holds a dear place in our hearts, maybe even more so than the Father. Jesus is the one who came to earth and told us about the plan of God, who redeemed us by his blood, who feeds us through the Eucharist. He's the one who intercedes for us before the throne of God.

But it seems more difficult to describe the Holy Spirit, the Third Person of the Trinity. For many of us, he remains a mysterious force. On one level, this is somewhat understandable. The images used to describe him—*fire, wind, rain,* and *dove*—may imply a vague notion rather than a living person with whom we can have a relationship. What's more, his primary mission is to reveal the Father and the Son to us, not himself. It's almost as if he enjoys working in the background. But that doesn't mean we can't identify his work in us or experience his power.

A Limited but Helpful Analogy

Let's use an analogy to help explain how the Spirit works. Picture your brain. It has two hemispheres, which work closely together. Scientists believe that one side of the brain governs our logical thinking; the other side governs our creative thinking. Then the nervous system ties these two halves together, coordinates all the impulses from them, and sends these impulses to the rest of the body, enabling us to take action as necessary.

Let's imagine the Father as the "left hemisphere" and Jesus as the "right hemisphere." We might then compare the Holy Spirit to the nervous system, revealing the will of the Father and the Son to us, energizing our bodies, and urging us to act in a godly way. Of course, this analogy is imperfect, but it does help us expand our understanding of the Holy Spirit and the vital role he plays in our lives. Like the way that the nervous system works, the Holy Spirit wants to take what is of God and communicate it to us. He wants to teach us, to move us, and to convince us of how much the whole Trinity cares for us.

Meeting the Holy Spirit

Throughout Scripture, the Holy Spirit is presented as having the attributes we associate with God the Father. Like the Father, he is eternal, having no beginning and no end (Hebrews 9:14). He is omnipresent, everywhere at the same time (Psalm 139:7). He is omniscient, having all knowledge and insight into the mystery of

God and his plan (1 Corinthians 2:10-11). He is omnipotent, being himself the "power of the Most High" (Luke 1:35).

Like the Father, the Holy Spirit is not distant, cold, or aloof. Rather, he is with us and lives in our hearts (1 Corinthians 3:16). He speaks to us (Acts 13:2); commands us (16:6); intercedes for us (Romans 8:26); leads us (8:14); testifies about Jesus to us (John 15:26); reveals the truth of Christ to us (16:13); convicts us of sin and final judgment (16:8, 11); convinces us that Jesus is the Lord of all creation (16:14-15); joins us and helps us pray to God (Romans 8:16); sanctifies us (15:16); and seals God's promises of eternal life in our hearts (Ephesians 1:13-14).

What a magnificent job description! And this list is far from complete. At first glance, all of these responsibilities seem over-whelming. How could the Spirit possibly accomplish all of this, and for so many people? We have only to look at the past two thou-sand years of church history—and the countless centuries before Christ—for the evidence!

The Spirit in the Church

It was the Spirit who came upon the church at Pentecost. It was the Spirit who moved Saul at Damascus. It was the Spirit who guided the development of the churches in Ephesus, Corinth, Thessalonica, Philippi, Galatia, and beyond. It was the Spirit who moved the Ethiopian eunuch, the jailer and his family, Lydia, and Cornelius to conversion and to a new life as members of the body of Christ.

It was the Spirit who moved the saints to conversion. Who can forget the sinner-turned-saint story of Augustine? Or the way the Spirit raised up St. Dominic to help combat heresy and spread the gospel? Or the way the Spirit used a somewhat complacent nun—Teresa of Avila—to spark a revival in prayer and spirituality that continues to affect the church today?

These stories of conversion, love, and service tell about different men and women who did something special for God. But they are also stories of how the Holy Spirit was doing his job. Of course, it was the men and women who decided to cooperate, but the Holy Spirit was always the guiding force, working behind the scenes to reveal God's will to them and to empower them beyond their natural human limitations.

The Spirit at Work

Today the Holy Spirit is still working among us. He is in all of us, urging us to live and work for God. Our lives are not just a combination of fate and lucky or unlucky circumstances. Rather, the Holy Spirit is always guiding us, always seeking to give us the wisdom and guidance of God our Father (1 Corinthians 2:7).

St. Thomas Aquinas taught that a person who is in a state of grace is open to the virtues and gifts that God has poured out. These virtues and gifts help us stay connected with God and give us the ability to hear from the Holy Spirit and to sense what he wants to reveal to us.

In the history of the church, we've seen the Holy Spirit lead saints to sacrifice and serve in dramatic ways. But there are many more everyday ways the Holy Spirit wants to lead us and draw us closer to God. Let's look at two key areas: the Spirit's work of convicting us of sin and his work of convincing us of Jesus' holiness, power, and lordship.

Convicting Us of Sin

On the night before he died, Jesus prophesied that Peter would deny him three times—which Peter did. Through hindsight, we can see that Jesus' prediction was not just a lucky guess. Rather, it was part of God's plan for Peter. Obviously, Peter had a free will and could have chosen not to deny Jesus. But somehow Jesus knew that fear and weak faith would overpower Peter's genuine love for the Lord. Far from a coincidence, Jesus' prediction and Peter's denial fit together as part of God's way of teaching Peter and forming in him the humility necessary to become the head of the church.

At first glance, we might think, *There's no way I can expect to receive such a clear and precise warning from the Holy Spirit.* Upon deeper reflection, we might come to a different conclusion. If we look at Peter's denial as just one instance of sin, we might say that Peter simply had a moment of weakness. Surely Jesus would not be surprised to see Peter fearing for his life. But let's consider this episode as part of a larger pattern.

Earlier Peter had rebuked Jesus for mentioning the cross—and received an even stronger rebuke himself (Matthew 16:21-23). A week later, at the transfiguration, Peter blurted out a proposal to keep Jesus, Moses, and Elijah on Mount Tabor, only to hear God tell him to be still and listen to Jesus (17:4-5). At the Last Supper, Peter tried to prevent Jesus from washing his feet before "switching gears" and saying, "Lord, not my feet only but also my hands and my head!" (John 13:9). Finally, at Jesus' arrest, Peter drew his sword and cut off the ear of the high priest's servant (18:10-11).

Again and again, Peter came face-to-face with his impetuous nature, which he couldn't change. We don't know how many more situations like this Peter had to go through, but we do know that he ultimately was transformed and chose to put his old nature to death and submit to God's wisdom.

Renewal by the Spirit's Power

This is how the Holy Spirit wants to work in our lives. He is less concerned with every individual sin we commit and more concerned with transforming us so we can become more like Jesus. To that end, he works patiently and compassionately, showing us the patterns of behavior that he wants to change.

If we look at Peter after Pentecost, we see a man who still had a strong, determined personality, but who was also humble and open to the Spirit. His impetuous behavior was transformed over time as he saw how much of a hindrance it was. And because he was open to the Spirit, Peter could come to a deeper and deeper repentance—a repentance that cleansed his conscience and transformed his mind.

Of all the ways the Spirit works to deliver us from sin and renew us, the most powerful is through the Sacrament of Reconciliation.

It's the gentle pricking of the Spirit that lifts our consciences to heaven and tells us that we need to go to confession. It's the compassion of the Spirit that convinces us that there is a way out of sin. It's the Spirit's cleansing that tells us that through this sacrament God has showered us with his mercy and forgiven us with his love. It's the grace of the Spirit that reminds us of Jesus' words: "Neither do I condemn you; go, and do not sin again" (John 8:11).

Spirit-Inspired Guilt

There is a huge difference between the guilt brought about by the Holy Spirit and the guilt that comes from the evil one. The Holy Spirit pricks us with guilt only to show us how our sin hurts our life with God. His goal is to move us to repentance so that we can be transformed.

Satan, on the other hand, pricks our consciences with an entirely different goal. He doesn't care about us. He only wants to hurt God by keeping us bound in guilt and failure. He wants to immobilize us and convince us that we simply don't have what it takes to follow Jesus faithfully.

So the next time you feel guilty, examine where your guilt is leading you and try to determine who is behind it.

The Holy Spirit will use every means possible to show us our sin so that we can change. He may speak to us in our prayer, at Mass, through a friend, or even on our way to work. Don't dismiss these promptings as mere coincidences! While a one-time, dramatic revelation can move us to repent, it's more likely that the Spirit will convict us over time, gradually unfolding the causes of sin—just as he did for Peter—transforming us from the inside out.

Convincing Us of Jesus' Lordship

When Jesus once asked his apostles, "Who do you say that I am?" (Matthew 16:15), Peter answered, "You are the Messiah, the Son of the living God" (16:16). Later, after his resurrection, Jesus appeared to his disciples. Face-to-face with the risen Christ, Thomas said simply, "My Lord and my God" (John 20:28). As dramatic as these stories are, they also reveal two truths for us today: First, the Holy Spirit wants to convince us that Jesus is our Lord and God, worthy of our worship and praise. Second, as he convinces us about Jesus, the Spirit also wants to transform us.

Just as the Holy Spirit uses the everyday events of life to reveal the areas that separate us from God and need to be transformed, the Spirit uses daily events to reveal the love, mercy, and power of Jesus so that we will surrender our lives to him more deeply.

The pattern for both kinds of revelation—convicting and convincing—is similar. The Spirit may reveal Jesus' love and power to us during Mass or when we are reading Scripture. He may use a comment from a spouse or a friend, or he may simply put a new thought into our minds. It may even happen when we are at odds with someone or when we are committing some sin. Remember, the Spirit touched Mary when she was in a state of perfect grace, but he also touched Paul when he was on his way to arrest and kill Christians.

The Spirit of Worship

Have you ever felt completely in love with Jesus, wanting to pour out every ounce of your being in worship? Have you ever been so caught up in prayer that you didn't care about the time or what was going on around you? Have you ever been so filled with his presence and so alive in the Spirit that you caught yourself thinking, *I wish I could leave this world and be with Jesus right now?*

These experiences are possible only because God created us with the capacity to know him deeply and personally. When the Holy Spirit moves in us and enlivens this spiritual capacity, we find ourselves lifted up to heaven and filled with the love of Jesus. We experience the "Spirit of adoption" flooding us and crying out, in accord with our own hearts, "Abba! Father!" (Romans 8:15-16). Of course, when we experience this, it's really our voice calling out in praise. It's our heart and our mind experiencing the love and responding with joy and gratitude. At the same time, by a mystery that we may never understand, the Holy Spirit is with us, praising God or bowing down in worship as well.

It's not a coincidence when we find ourselves in God's presence. It doesn't just happen. When we sense the presence of the Lord, and when we feel his love, it's the Holy Spirit at work, convincing us that Jesus is our Savior and our Lord.

Again and again, the Holy Spirit wants to fill us with his joy and with the peace of Christ. These are not just snappy catchwords; they describe the Spirit's desire to make us alive to God. They explain what happens when the Spirit takes what Jesus taught—and all the blessings the Father has for us—and imparts them to us. And whenever this happens, we are moved to worship Jesus from our hearts.

Praying in the Spirit

Scripture says, "Build yourselves up on your most holy faith; pray in the Holy Spirit; keep yourselves in the love of God" (Jude 20-21). And in another place: "Pray in the Spirit at all times in every prayer and supplication" (Ephesians 6:18). There is a vital link between the Holy Spirit and prayer, and especially between the Holy Spirit and our ability to experience Jesus' love in prayer—directly, powerfully, and transformingly. But the question arises: what does it mean to "pray in the Spirit"?

We can explain this through the "eighty-twenty" rule. Learning how to pray in the Spirit can be a challenge. At first, our prayer may be 80 percent our effort, with the remaining 20 percent being the Spirit's power. But as we persevere over time, we find ourselves laboring less and less, to the point where our prayer is 80 percent the Spirit's work and only 20 percent our work. We find ourselves enjoying God's presence and his grace more and more as the Holy Spirit takes over our times of communion with God. This change doesn't happen overnight, and it isn't always a smooth transition. But God will reward our efforts.

The Gift Giver

Prayer is not the only way the Spirit works to convince us that Jesus is Lord. In addition to helping us pray, the Spirit wants to give us gifts that will help us grow closer to God and empower us to build up the church. Through his "sanctifying gifts"—wisdom, understanding, counsel, fortitude, knowledge, piety, and fear of the Lord—the Spirit forms and renews our character so that we are more open to his revelations. As "permanent dispositions" of the heart, these gifts help keep the lines of communication open between us and God and make us more trusting when it comes to following his will (Isaiah 11:1-2; *Catechism of the Catholic Church,* 1830–31).

The "charismatic gifts"—wisdom, knowledge, faith, healing, miracles, prophecy, discernment, tongues, and interpretation of tongues—are geared less toward our own personal development and more toward the common good and the state of the church (1 Corinthians 12:7-11). The Spirit gives us these gifts so that we might pray for a person's healing, seek God's wisdom on a thorny issue, discern what the Spirit might be saying, or exercise supernatural faith in God's power and love for the world.

Finally, the fruit of the Spirit—love, joy, peace, patience, kindness, goodness, gentleness, faithfulness, and self-control (Galatians 5:22-23)—are both a work in progress and a witness. They are a work in progress because they are the character elements that the Holy Spirit is always building within us. He is always at work replacing division with peace, selfishness with goodness, and anxiety with joy. They are a witness because the testimony of these fruits in our lives is a kind of proof that the Spirit is at work in us and that we are accepting his grace and putting it into practice.

Admittedly, this is a very limited presentation on the gifts and fruit of the Spirit. But it can help reinforce the point that the Holy Spirit is with us, always reaching out to us. He uses these gifts and fruit to convince us that Jesus is far more powerful and far more loving than we can ever imagine. He also gives us these gifts to help us in our daily living so that as we grow and mature, we become more and more convinced that Jesus is Lord of all.

So don't be afraid to ask for—and to use—the gifts of the Holy Spirit. While it does take time to develop them, trust that the Spirit is in you; know that you are capable of receiving his gifts. They were poured into you at your baptism, and God is just waiting for you to embrace them.

Praying with the Holy Spirit

St. Paul told the Corinthians that they were a temple of the Holy Spirit and that through this Spirit they had the mind of Christ and could be taught by him (1 Corinthians 2:14-16; 6:19). He prayed that the Ephesians would receive "a spirit of wisdom and revelation" (Ephesians 1:17). And he told the Colossians that God had chosen to reveal to them the great mystery of Christianity: "Christ in you, the hope of glory" (Colossians 1:27).

These words—and similar ones found in almost all of Paul's letters—tell us that the Holy Spirit is among us, always seeking to convince us that Jesus is Lord. This truth is the very foundation for our faith. So with expectant hearts, let's take every opportunity to open ourselves to the Holy Spirit. He wants to energize us with his grace and replace apathy and hopelessness with joy and vision.

The Spirit at Work in You

Proverbs 24:3-4 says that "by wisdom a house is built, and by understanding it is established; by knowledge the rooms are filled with all precious and pleasant riches." This is what the Holy Spirit wants to do in all of us as we learn the art—and the blessings—of worship.

Entering into worship requires us to quiet our minds. So as you start to pray, imagine yourself leaving the world behind you and passing through a large gate that leads to heaven's courtyard. Imagine yourself entering this gate with thanksgiving and coming into this courtyard with praise (Psalm 100:4).

One way to experience the Spirit's blessings that come from worship is to dwell on the great things God has done. You may want to focus on the beauty and perfection of creation, on your own personal blessings, or on Jesus himself.

Your worship can also be enlivened as you meditate on Scripture. Read a parable or a miracle story or a description of the New Jerusalem. Ask the Holy Spirit to help you grasp the love of Jesus or the wisdom of the Father.

Walking through the Stations of the Cross or praying the rosary is another way to contemplate the mysteries of Jesus. It gives you the added benefit of praising God with your heart, your mind, and your body.

Every day, try to set aside a few moments just for Jesus. Follow some of the suggestions above and see what the Holy Spirit says to you and does in your heart. When you have finished, write down what you sensed. It may seem that your journal entry came from your mind, but don't rule out the possibility that the Holy Spirit was at work.

As you meditate on the greatness of God, it may feel as if it is mostly your effort. But in time, you will notice a change. You may feel a greater love for God or for your family. You may find yourself becoming more patient or generous. You may want to spend more time in prayer or reading Scripture. As this happens, it's because what began as 80 percent your effort and 20 percent reliance upon God's grace shifted to become more like 80 percent God's work in you and 20 percent your effort. And that means that you are striving less and receiving more!

CHAPTER 9

MARY: A MIRROR OF FAITH AND MYSTERY

When the Son of God entered the world, he didn't simply appear one day in a blaze of glory, bringing immediate salvation. In God's perfect plan, his Son was "born of woman, born under the law, to redeem those who were under the law, so that we might receive adoption as sons" (Galatians 4:4-5).

The woman's name was Mary, destined by God to bring his Son into the world, destined to be the vessel of divine life and the one through whom the eternal God would enter the world to redeem it.

Imagine how important the character of the mother of the Son of God must be. She was chosen to sum up—in her heart and in her deeds—Israel's centuries-old longing for God's promises to be fulfilled. She was destined to give birth to, nurture, and train the One who would save all people from sin! She was the one who would become the model for all Christians throughout the centuries, teaching by her example and helping to bring about by her intercession the purity of heart and singleness of mind that God desires in all his children.

As we consider Mary's journey of faith and then look at the specific roles she played, we can see in her a mirror of faith but far more than that as well: a mirror of mystery.

Mary's Journey of Faith

From the moment of the angel's visit, Mary began a journey of faith that brought her to an ever-deeper experience of God's love. Every challenge, every obstacle, every threat to her peace gave her the opportunity to trust God more completely and to allow the Spirit to pour more love into her heart. The more we come to understand how the Spirit moved Mary and formed her, the more we can understand the Spirit's actions in our own lives. By looking at Mary's journey of faith and the way she responded to the challenges placed before her, we can see how the Spirit can form these same dispositions of discipleship in our hearts as well.

Growing up as a daughter of Israel, Mary would have been intimately familiar with God's promises concerning the Messiah; like her people, she too hungered for the Redeemer to come. How fervently she must have prayed with her fellow Israelites, "How long, O LORD?" (Psalm 13:1; see also 90:13), waiting and hoping for the promised salvation!

Mary's heart seemed ripe to receive the good news. And yet when Gabriel appeared to her, Mary was "greatly troubled" by his greeting (Luke 1:29). The angel told her that she was to conceive miraculously and bear a child who would be called "holy, the Son of God" (1:35). Her child would "save his people from their sins" (Matthew 1:21). Despite all the preparation in Mary's heart—even despite her sinless purity, being free from the taint of original sin—the angel's appearance confronted her with an unexpected challenge. She was being invited by Almighty God to participate in his plan of salvation, and in a way marvelous beyond imagining!

Mary could not grasp why God would choose someone like herself to fulfill such a mission. And although she was probably familiar with Isaiah's words that a young woman would conceive and bear a child called Immanuel—"God with us"—the notion that she would conceive by the power of the Spirit was still too incredible to grasp.

Although Mary's mind could not fully grasp this revelation, her faith and love for God enabled her to say yes. Despite the questions that must have entered her mind, Mary knew that God was trustworthy. This humble "handmaid of the Lord" chose to remain faithful to God. In her *fiat*—"Let it be to me according to your word" (Luke 1:38)—this daughter of Israel inaugurated a new era in God's design. His promised redemption—the new, unbreakable covenant—was to be finally brought to pass. In Mary's womb, her people's longing for Christ was fulfilled.

As the angel left her, Mary's journey of faith became an adventure that was to surpass anything she could have envisioned.

Pondering and Preparing, Treasuring and Testing

We can trace Mary's journey of faith by looking at the different journeys she made during her life. Once the angel left her, Mary "went with haste into the hill country, to a city of Judah" (Luke 1:39), to visit Elizabeth, her kinswoman, who had conceived the herald of the Messiah. This being at least a three-day journey, Mary had time to think and pray. We can picture her recalling her encounter with the angel, as the Spirit prepared her heart more deeply for her role in God's plan. At Elizabeth's home, Mary's prayer of praise and gratitude—the Magnificat—welled up from a heart deeply touched by the Spirit (1:46-55).

Luke repeatedly portrays Mary quietly pondering the things that she witnessed and treasuring them in her heart (see Luke 1:29; 2:19, 51). This was not an anxiety-laden attempt to make sense out of confusing circumstances. Rather, Mary turned to God for understanding. She opened her heart to God and asked him to teach her more about this Messiah, conceived by the Spirit, who was to be her son. As a result, even as Jesus was growing physically in Mary's womb, he was also growing spiritually in her heart.

Even before Jesus' birth, God began to show Mary the kind of reception the world would provide for her son. Although there could have been numerous reasons why "there was no place for them in the inn" at Bethlehem (Luke 2:7), Luke paints this scene to foreshadow the rejection that Jesus would face in his public ministry. Angels heralded his birth, but only to "unimportant" shepherds. From the very start, Jesus was welcomed by the humble and opposed by the powerful.

At Jesus' presentation in the temple, Mary received a foretaste of the effect that this rejection would have on her. The aged Simeon— who had longed to see the promised Messiah—prophesied that Jesus was destined to be a "sign that is spoken against." In the next breath, he told Mary, "A sword will pierce through your own soul" (Luke 2:34-35). So at the very beginning of her life as the mother of the Christ, Mary faced the mystery of the cross. The redemption she longed and prayed for would cost her and her son dearly.

The signs of Jesus' rejection increased. To avoid Herod's murderous rage, Mary and Joseph fled to Egypt (Matthew 2:13-15). They became refugees, retracing the journey of the children of Israel fleeing Pharaoh's wrath. In her flight, Mary faced another stage in her journey, and a more difficult one at that. He who had visited her so graciously through the angel was now testing and strengthening her, calling her to a deeper trust. And because she submitted to the Lord, Mary grew in the strength that comes from humble surrender and prayerful reflection.

During the hidden years before Jesus' public ministry, Mary's love for God must have deepened as she told her son the circumstances surrounding his birth. Throughout this time, the Spirit was at work in Mary, clarifying her understanding of who Jesus was. In prayer, she pondered the scriptural promises, asked God for wisdom, and closely watched her son grow strong in the Spirit as he approached the time of his ministry.

The Time Is Fulfilled

The Gospel of John begins and ends Jesus' public ministry with two events involving Mary. First, at the wedding feast of Cana (2:1-11), Jesus seemed reluctant to perform any miracles. But it was his mother's disposition of faith and trust that moved him to begin his ministry. In humility, Mary persisted in prayerful expectancy that God would grant her heart's desire.

Mary had begun to understand her son's mission and was eager for his work to begin. Years earlier, the angel had told her that Jesus would inherit the kingdom of David (Luke 1:32-33); now she longed to see this kingdom come. While Jesus knew it was not yet the "hour" when he would be glorified on the cross (John 2:4), he yielded to her request, performing a miracle that pointed to the longing in both their hearts for the eternal "wedding banquet."

Second, Mary was present at the end of Jesus' ministry—on Calvary, where she witnessed the fulfillment of Simeon's prophecy (John 19:25-27). As Mary watched her son's agony, did the angel's hopeful promises seem meaningless and empty to her? Jesus was supposed to be "great . . . the Son of the Most High. . . . Of his kingdom there [would] be no end" (Luke 1:32-33). How was she to understand this? "Standing at the foot of the cross, Mary is the witness, humanly speaking, of the complete negation of these words." Yet, "How completely she abandons herself to God without reserve" (Pope John Paul II, *Mother of the Redeemer,* 18).

Mary's journey of faith had taken her down roads she never expected to travel. Through trials and joys, she watched the Father's plan unfold, and she willingly played the part God had marked out for her. Even though her heart was pierced with anguish, she never once cursed God or abandoned her calling. Even as she held her son's dead body, Mary knew that it must be this way. All the years of prayer and openness to the Spirit had taught her that this man's death would bring life to the world. The kingdom she longed for had come, and she had only to wait for Easter to see all her hopes fulfilled and her sorrows reversed.

The Mirror of Faith

While playing a special role in God's plan, Mary remained a humble, lowly believer. From her conception she was graced with the merits of Jesus' cross—freedom from the bondage of sin. Yet she still faced real, human choices and felt real, human emotions. Her triumph was one of faith—the same faith available to each of us.

Another way to treasure Mary's example is to look at how the four Evangelists portray her in the gospels. By exploring these different portraits, we can gain a deeper appreciation of Mary and the essential role she played—and continues to play—in God's plan of salvation. Again in each of the gospels, we see in her a mirror of faith.

Four Gospel Portraits of Mary

The four gospels were written at different times for different communities. Although they all present the revealed truth of salvation through Christ, each highlights a different aspect of the good news. Likewise, each gospel account emphasizes one aspect of Mary's role as well: as the virgin mother of God, as a member of the Holy Family, as a disciple of Jesus, and as the mother of the church.

Mark: Mary as Disciple

Mark's gospel was probably written about A.D. 65, and its goal was to encourage Christians, primarily of gentile origin, to become and remain true disciples of Jesus. Because Mark's gospel begins with the public life of Jesus, it contains only two direct references to Mary.

In Mark 3:31-35, as Jesus was teaching a crowd, he was told that his mother and other relatives were outside, asking for him. (The traditional Semitic phrase *brothers and sisters* refers to relatives of varying degrees, including nephews, nieces, cousins.) Jesus responded: "Here are my mother and my brothers! Whoever does the will of God is my brother, and sister, and mother." Jesus' answer may seem shocking at first, but a closer look reveals the essence of discipleship. It also, surprisingly, places Mary at the heart of this calling. She was the first one to "do the will of God" when she embraced God's invitation to be the mother of his Son.

In the second account, Mark 6:1-6, Jesus was rejected in his hometown of Nazareth. His former neighbors, scandalized at his new ministry, asked, "Where did this man get all this? . . . Is not this the carpenter, the son of Mary?" Mark continues: "He could do no mighty work there. . . . And he marveled because of their unbelief."

In both scenes, Mary was humble and quiet. Her special dignity was veiled, even when her call to discipleship was clearly indicated. This first of disciples remained hidden, seeking no glory or attention. Her only joy was in doing God's will.

Matthew: Mary in the Holy Family

Matthew's gospel, written around A.D. 85 (perhaps in Syria) for a mostly Jewish-Christian audience, focuses on the formation of a new community in Jesus as the fulfillment of the hope of the Old Testament. Matthew 1:23 makes explicit reference to Isaiah's prophecy (7:14) that a virgin (or young woman) would conceive and bear a son called Immanuel. For Matthew, Mary belonged within the community of the Holy Family, under the guidance of Joseph. Her place reflects Matthew's emphasis on the love and freedom that should be central to the life of the church.

Throughout Matthew's portrait of Mary, the spotlight falls primarily on Jesus and Joseph. Mary's task is to support the unity and love that are vital in every family and in the church. We see this theme depicted in Joseph's dilemma, when he discovered that his intended wife was pregnant. Because Mary had chosen to obey God's call—even at the risk of losing Joseph—God sent an angel to help Joseph decide to continue his role as protector and provider for this chosen woman and her child.

Matthew speaks of the centrality of the family again when he portrays the wise men coming to pay homage to the newborn king of the Jews at the home of Mary and Joseph (2:10-11). Mary was privileged to witness the promised faith of the gentiles (see Isaiah 60:1-3), even as she cared for her family. The theme is sounded again when Mary's family flees into Egypt (Matthew 2:13-15). Just as the Old Testament Joseph was sold into slavery in Egypt and ended up saving his family from famine (Genesis 45:4-8), so Mary's husband fled to Egypt—not only to preserve the child entrusted to him, but also to protect the entire church that would come to birth through this child's mission.

Luke: Virgin Mother of God Incarnate

Luke probably wrote from Antioch around A.D. 85, to converts from pagan religions within the Roman Empire. Luke places Mary in the tradition of Israelite women that included Abraham's wife Sarah (Genesis 18:1-15; 21:1-7); the unnamed mother of Samson (Judges 13:2-5, 24); and Hannah, Samuel's mother (1 Samuel 1:1-2, 9-20). These women conceived miraculously and mothered men of God who foreshadowed Christ, both in character and mission.

There is something special in Luke's portrayal of Mary. He seems to penetrate her character and show us more of her human qualities, attributes that could guide us as well: her humility, generosity, faith, and joy; her life of prayer; her maternal instincts.

When she heard about her older cousin Elizabeth's pregnancy, Mary "went with haste" to her side, to share her joy and to be of service (Luke 1:39). When Elizabeth praised her faith, Mary replied with the Magnificat, a hymn that glorified the Lord's holiness, justice, and mercy (1:46-55). Like Hannah (1 Samuel 1–2), Mary recognized that despite her "low estate," all generations would call her blessed because of the great things the Lord had done in her (Luke 1:48-49). Humility always acknowledges the truth—even of one's own blessedness—a central theme in Luke (see 10:19-20).

At Bethlehem, Mary gave birth to Jesus, tenderly caring for his needs despite their lack of basic accommodations (Luke 2:7). After shepherds arrived, talking of an angelic announcement, Mary pondered their sayings (2:19). Such a prayerful disposition no doubt prepared her to receive Simeon's words, at Jesus' presentation in the

Temple: "A sword will pierce through your own soul also" (2:35).

When Mary and Joseph found the twelve-year-old Jesus in the temple, Mary expressed her concern: "Son, why have you treated us so? Behold, your father and I have been looking for you anxiously" (Luke 2:48). Even when Jesus explained himself, they did not understand his words. But Mary "kept all these things in her heart" (2:50-51). Mary had said yes to the angel at the annunciation, and here, twelve years later, she had the opportunity to deepen that yes by accepting her son's mission in a fuller way.

Luke completes his portrait of Mary with two quick scenes (8:19-21; 11:27-28) in which Jesus' words seem to be a rejection of Mary: "My mother and my brothers are those who hear the word of God and do it"; and "Blessed rather are those who hear the word of God and keep it." Mary probably understood Jesus' meaning more than anyone else who heard them. Time and again, she had shown herself to be a faithful hearer and observer of God's word. That is why Luke goes out of his way to mention Mary's presence at Pentecost in Acts 1:14. She had been overshadowed by the Holy Spirit at the annunciation. Now she received the Spirit once again, both for her own guidance and for that of the church.

John: Mother of the Church

Written in Asia Minor around A.D. 95, John's gospel presents the human-divine mystery of Jesus in all its profound depth and glory. As we noted above, John speaks of Mary only twice, once toward the beginning of his gospel and once toward the end. In both scenes, Mary was involved in the lives of others besides Jesus, but in union with him.

As recorded in John 2, Mary told Jesus that the hosts of a wedding banquet they were attending had run out of wine. Though his answer seemed to rebuke her, she confidently instructed the stewards: "Do whatever he tells you" (2:3, 5). Evidently Jesus' hour had arrived, occasioned by Mary's intercession and persevering faith. By turning the water into wine, Jesus created a powerful symbol of his message, that the reign of God was being inaugurated as a joyful messianic banquet. All this at Mary's initiative!

When Jesus—on the cross—told the beloved disciple, "Behold, your mother" (John 19:26-27), he was entrusting Mary to this disciple's care, but as a "mother." This unnamed beloved disciple represents the whole Christian community, so at her son's request, Mary became mother of the church. In John's gospel, Mary is a new Eve, for in both scenes she was addressed as "woman" (2:4; 19:26), an allusion to the "woman" at Adam's side (Genesis 2:23), "the mother of all living" (3:20).

This allusion is seen again in the Book of Revelation, where John speaks of a woman in labor whose unborn child is threatened by a dragon or a serpent (12:1-9). When the child is born, he is safely taken up to the throne of God, while the woman flees into the wilderness. Many believers through the centuries have come to see this woman as Mary, the new Eve, whose offspring would triumph over the ancient serpent whose deception led humanity into sin (see Genesis 3:15-16).

A Mirror of the Mystery

Mary's person and vocation mirror the mystery of Jesus and the mystery of our own lives. Like Mary, we too are disciples called to follow Jesus in faith, love, and service. By telling her story in four different ways, the gospels give us a multifaceted view of the richness of her life and all that she offers to the church. Whether we see her as the first disciple, as a member of the Holy Family, as the virgin mother of God incarnate, or as the mother of the church, we can honor and admire her, follow her counsels, and call her sister, mother, and friend.

Mary's Continuing Role

Mary continues to invite every disciple of Jesus to follow his example. Mary was in the upper room on Pentecost, as the final age of the church was inaugurated. All throughout this age, Mary continues to fulfill God's purposes for her. Just as she did at Cana, she continues to intercede with her son. In the past two centuries especially, she has shown her concern through various apparitions in which the Mother of God speaks to the children of God. Whether the messages in these apparitions concern turning away from sin or receiving God's love in prayer, they seem to focus on preparing the world for Jesus' return at the end of time. She has often appeared weeping over the world's sin and imploring people to repent and seek her son.

For example, when she appeared to Catherine Labouré in 1830, Mary spoke a twofold message of grace and judgment: "My child, the times are very evil. Sorrows will befall France; the throne will be overturned. The whole world will be plunged into every kind of misery. But come to the foot of the altar. There graces will be shed upon all, great and small, who ask for them."

Recounting her later vision of the Miraculous Medal, Catherine said: "It made me realize how right it was to pray to the Blessed Virgin and how generous she was to those who did pray to her, what graces she gave to those who asked for them, what joy she had in giving them." Just as she willingly directed the stewards at Cana toward her son (John 2:5), so even now Mary rejoices in leading God's people back to him.

We can also see Mary's eagerness to bring people to the Lord in the story of her appearance to Bernadette at Lourdes. For some 150 years, pilgrims have flocked to this French village, thousands of them healed and brought to conversion and a deeper experience of God's love.

And during World War I Mary appeared to nine-year-old Lucia Abobora and her two cousins in Fatima, Portugal, to urge them to pray for those lost in sin. In one vision, Mary showed the children the pain and anguish experienced by those in hell. They were like "coals in a fiery furnace, with never an instant's peace or freedom." In all her appearances to them, Mary urged the children to pray that many would be saved from sin as they repent and put their faith in her son.

Like Mary, God invites all of us on a pilgrimage of faith. He wants us to listen to his voice in our hearts, to ponder his word in Scripture. Mary has given us a beautiful example of what it means to yield to God. She has taught us to treasure God's voice and to allow the Holy Spirit to guide us. As Jesus' first disciple, she prayed, "Let it be done to me according to your word"—a prayer each of us can learn to say with ever-increasing trust. Through the power of the Spirit, we can long for Jesus to come again, just as Mary prayed for his first appearance. With hope and confidence, let us take up our mission on earth as we await the coming kingdom and the full unveiling of the Father's plan for every man and woman.

CHAPTER 10

DISCOVERING THE LORD
WHO HEALS

Two thousand years ago, Jesus walked all over the Holy Land healing people of their illnesses and restoring their wounded hearts. According to the Gospel of Matthew, Jesus went throughout Galilee "healing every disease and every sickness among the people" (Matthew 4:23). Mark tells us that wherever Jesus went, people "laid the sick in the marketplaces, and begged him that they might touch even the fringe of his cloak; and all who touched it were healed" (Mark 6:56). It seems that healing was an everyday part of Jesus' ministry—one of the most powerful signs that the kingdom of God had come.

Healing is one area that seems to be enjoying a kind of revival in recent years. At healing Masses, at prayer gatherings, and even in the confessional, people are crying out to God, asking him to heal their inner wounds and take away their infirmities. Healings such as those recorded in Scripture and documented at places such as Lourdes and Fatima now seem to be taking place all over the world. What's more, fewer people are holding the idea that sickness is a sign of punishment from God. Even the notion that God wants us to endure pain and sickness as a way of suffering with Christ has been clarified to include the possibility of healing from God.

Do you believe that God wants to heal his people today? Don't be afraid to challenge your doubts or preconceptions. When we take our faith personally, we believe that God will do what he has promised. We have expectant faith that he really does have the power to heal us. If you've never done so before, try implementing some of the suggestions in this chapter for healing prayer, both for inner healing and for physical healing. Know, too, that whatever the outcome of your prayer, your faith in Jesus and his loving plan for your life will be strengthened simply because you have spent time with him in prayer.

Witnesses to God's Healing Power

When Jesus came to inaugurate the kingdom of God, he healed people as signs that this kingdom was at hand. Today, his kingdom *has* come, and he still wants to heal his people. Over the past thirty years, many Catholics have been privileged to see many dramatic healings occur when people have prayed together for someone, whether at parish missions, in their homes, or at prayer meetings.

For example, one man had a broken blood vessel in his eye, causing blurred vision. After several Catholics on a mission prayer team placed their hands on him and prayed for about twenty minutes, the bleeding stopped and his eye cleared.

On another occasion, a woman who had gone through an ugly divorce a year earlier asked for prayer at a parish mission. Although she had gone to confession, she was still plagued with feelings of guilt and shame. A team couple prayed with her for about an hour, and she gradually felt God's healing power. Over the next few evenings, the couple encouraged her to picture Jesus coming into the room and ministering to her personally. As she did, a mountain of guilt dissolved. While the reality of her divorce will never go away, this woman did experience Jesus freeing her from her pain and her haunting sense of failure.

At a prayer meeting dedicated to healing, one woman reluctantly asked for prayer. Feeling that many people needed more significant healing than she did, she was embarrassed to make her request: to ask God to take away her springtime allergies. Amazing as it sounds, with prayer her sneezing and other symptoms disappeared.

Jesus Wants to Heal

These examples can encourage us not to rely on "good reason" so much that we disregard the hope that Jesus may want to work a wonder in our lives. Of course, we should always take advantage of the skills of a medical doctor; yet at the same time, we should ask Jesus, the great physician, to pour out his healing balm on our lives.

If you are suffering from a physical illness or an inner wound, don't just assume it's a "cross" that Jesus wants you to bear. It may be, but then again it may not. Unless you have a specific sense from God that he is asking you to share in Jesus' redemptive suffering, there's no reason why you shouldn't pray expectantly for Jesus to heal you. Far too often, we Catholics have said, "I will embrace this cross and I will suffer through its demands." Yet Scripture indicates that the vast majority of people who came to Jesus were healed and restored.

Can you imagine a child bringing a need to his parents, only to be told that it's not worth their time or attention? Likewise, no wound in your life is too small for God. Be like Bartimaeus and cry out to the Lord. Be like Jairus and ask for what seems impossible. Be like the centurion and intercede for your loved ones. Seek Jesus in prayer and believe that he wants to heal you because he loves you. Believe Jesus' promise that those who ask, receive; those who seek, find; and those who knock are blessed to see the door of healing open.

A Fresh Outpouring

One of the most promising truths of the gospel is that you don't have to have a pronounced and powerful gift in order to see healing happen. Jesus doesn't limit his power to people named Francis of Assisi or Catherine of Seina. A false humility can prompt us to think that we aren't good enough to be his instruments of healing; nothing could be further from the truth. The power is his, not ours, and he can use any one of us to reach out to the wounded and hurting.

Praying for Inner Healing

There is such brokenness in the world! So many people walk around with inner wounds, just begging for a chance at freedom. God wants to heal painful memories. He wants to remove lingering guilt, shame, or failure that keeps his people from living as witnesses to his love and power. Those on parish missions and prayer teams have found that when an opportunity for prayer is offered, many of the people who come forward tend to ask for inner healing more often than they ask for physical healing.

The Sources of Suffering

There is a great need for healing of inner wounds, whatever their source. Some wounds are simply the result of living in this fallen world. Even Jesus suffered internally. He wept, for example, at the tomb of his friend Lazarus and lamented over the hardness of heart of the people of Jerusalem. On another front, some of our suffering is the result of our own sin or pattern of sin. In this case, we need to accept Jesus' call to repent, receive his grace, and try to change our ways. But as difficult as these hardships may be, the dominant portion of our suffering is linked to painful memories caused by the emotional wounds from our past.

God wants us to know that, with his help, we can face the normal sufferings of life. He wants to convince us that our sinful ways can be changed. But most of all, he wants us to know that the wounds that have lodged themselves in our memories can be healed. If we want to experience these promises firsthand, we must learn how to trust Jesus. We all have at least a "mustard seed's" worth of faith. Don't we owe it to ourselves—and to Jesus—to ask our Savior to show us how much he longs to heal us?

Praying for Inner Healing

When we try to deal with our inner hurts in our own strength, we can make some progress. We can try to rise above our hurts and forgive those who have hurt us. We can try to maintain a peaceful attitude. Yet our efforts can take us only so far. This is especially true when the wound is deep and painful. At times like these—when we run up against our human limitations—we need to ask Jesus for his power and grace.

How do we pray for inner healing? The suggestions in this chapter are not intended to replace professional counseling where it is necessary. What is offered is simply a prayer pattern that can help you to overcome internal hurts. It's best to ask your spouse, a close friend of the same gender, or your pastor to join you and support you in this prayer. You may feel more comfortable asking a group of close friends to join you, as well.

Express Your Need

Sit in a quiet place with a spouse, a close friend, or a group of people you trust. Start by stating your need for healing. Tell the person(s) praying with you what happened to cause you to feel so wounded. Explain the situation and its effects on you as clearly as you can. Many of us find it difficult to be this open. We think, *It was so painful when it first happened; why do I have to relive it?* Yet experience shows that much healing can occur simply by bringing our wounds into the light and sharing them with a close friend.

Try to overcome your fears about sharing your past hurts. Begin by dealing with the small hurts, and see how God works.

Welcome Jesus

After sharing your need for healing, it's time to pray. Ask your prayer partner(s) to help you imagine yourself back at the time when the painful incident occurred. Recall the situation in as much detail as you can, only this time invite Jesus to be with you, observing everything as it happened. As you relive the incident, pay close attention to Jesus as well as the situation. Try to picture the expression of love on his face.

Now imagine yourself sitting with Jesus immediately after the painful incident. Again, look closely at Jesus' face, the compassion in his eyes, his look of concern and understanding. You may even see him putting his arm around your shoulder or holding your hand and looking into your eyes. You might repeat the name of Jesus or thank him for his love. Ask Jesus over and over to remove the pain. Give him the freedom to do whatever he needs to do to heal this memory. Jesus knows what you've experienced, and he is able to go back into the past with you and heal the sting and the pain in your memory.

Seeing Healing in Your Prayer

Next incorporate into this picture the person(s) with whom you need to be reconciled. Asking Jesus to help you, imagine yourself going to that person; say or do whatever Jesus inspires you to do. You may feel led to ask that person to forgive you, or you may picture the other person asking for your forgiveness. You may see Jesus with his arms around both of you, taking away your pain, healing your relationship, and giving you renewed hope. You may even feel a weight of resentment being lifted.

Remember

We can't always tell whether the thoughts that come to us in these times of prayer are from God or from our own imaginations. However, if the thoughts give you a sense of peace or a desire to forgive and be reconciled, don't discount the possibility that they come from God. On the other hand, if you find yourself focusing on how deep your hurt was, on seeking revenge, or on why the other person should come to you first, it's probably a sign that you need some more time to let the Lord's healing take place. Don't worry. Jesus is far more patient with us than we tend to be with ourselves. He will give you more time, and he will give you more opportunities to take further steps toward healing.

An Example of Healing Prayer

One man wanted prayer because he had been deeply hurt by members of his parish Bible study who had shunned him because of his stance on a social issue. The man said that he would swing between tears of sorrow and angry outbursts against these men in his parish.

The team praying with him asked Jesus to come into the room with him. The man was asked to imagine Jesus putting his arm around him and pouring his love upon him.

Next the man was invited to imagine the other men from his Bible study in the room. "Can you see that Jesus loves them too?" the team members asked. Finally, they all imagined Jesus as a mediator, holding the hand of the man as he also held the hands of the other men.

As the team prayed this way, the man felt a deep sense of release. He was able to forgive the other men, and the memory lost its bite. The pain that had been so real to him was now greatly reduced because of Jesus' power to heal.

You Can Do It

Praying for inner healing is relatively simple because Jesus does most of the work. It may seem like nothing more than a harmless exercise based in popular psychology, but we shouldn't underestimate the way such prayer opens us up to the miraculous and powerful grace of God. He knows our hearts and our intentions. We may feel as if we hardly know what we're doing, but we can trust that if our hearts are in the right place, our Father in heaven will heal us in ways we can't even imagine.

Time and again, people have been witness to inner healing. Jesus brings peace to troubled hearts. He pours out his healing balm. Don't be afraid to reach out to him.

Praying for Physical Healing

Many people find it easy to accept that God wants to bring them inner healing. But when it comes to physical healing, we tend to be a bit more skeptical. After all, the results of inner healing—which often manifest themselves over time—are not nearly as black and white as physical healing.

Too often, we doubt that God would want to use us as his instruments of healing. We doubt God, even though we have read stories in the Bible of "regular people" performing miraculous healings. One way to help overcome these doubts is to pray for physical healing on a small level, to pray for small things such as headaches, a child's cuts and scrapes, stomach-aches, and the like.

The Healing Power of Love

In spite of our doubts, we should devote as much time and energy to physical healing as we do to spiritual healing. Whether the infirmity is serious or minor, and whether a healing has occurred or not, the person who has received prayers is almost always deeply moved—encouraged, strengthened, and filled with hope—by the compassion of the prayer team. It would seem that the love flowing from the prayer team has its own healing effects.

The Mystery of Suffering

We don't know why God heals in some instances and not in others. Someday, we will find out. Until then, it will remain part of the mystery of Christ, something we aren't able to understand with our limited minds.

St. Paul had a powerful gift of healing. According to Scripture, when articles of clothing that had touched his skin were brought to the sick, "their diseases left them" (Acts 19:12). Yet no matter how gifted he was, Paul couldn't heal Timothy's stomach problem (1 Timothy 5:23). He couldn't heal Trophimus at Miletus (2 Timothy 4:20) or Epaphroditus in Rome (Philippians 2:25-27). Paul himself had a "physical infirmity" (Galatians 4:13), and he suffered from a "thorn in the flesh," which God did not heal (2 Corinthians 12:7-9). Were any of these instances of sickness caused by sin or a lack of faith? Probably not. These were men of faith who had accepted what God gave them and trusted God's will for their lives.

Ask, Seek, Knock

On the other hand, just praying "Lord, let your will be done" may breed an attitude that limits what God might want to do. Would Bartimaeus have been healed if he had not cried out to Jesus (Mark 10:46-48)? Would Lazarus have been raised from the dead if his sisters had not asked Jesus to come (John 11:3)? And Jairus, who fell at Jesus' feet and begged him to heal his daughter (Luke 8:41-42): would that healing have occurred without his intercession?

These stories—and so many like them—tell us that the spiritual principle of calling on Jesus applies to our physical, as much as to our spiritual, needs. When Jesus told us to ask, seek, and knock, he didn't intend to restrict it to spiritual issues. God wants us to ask for healing. "I am the LORD who heals you" (Exodus 15:26).

How often should we ask for physical healing? All the time—for big things as well as for little ones. We can go so far as to say that we should persevere until there is a sense that a person is near the time of death and that God is calling that person home. Until then, it's good and right to pray for physical healing. Praying for healing is like a garden receiving sunlight. The more prayer (or sunlight) a person is exposed to, the more healing (warmth, nourishment, and strength) he or she receives.

If you are sick, or are praying for someone who is sick, follow the advice of Scripture. Call on the members of your family or the leaders of your parish and ask them to pray with you and anoint you in the name of the Lord. "The prayer of faith will save the sick, and the Lord will raise them up" (James 5:15).

Looking Beyond Human Solutions

Mark 5:25-34 tells the story of a woman who had been bleeding for twelve years. She had consulted many doctors, and she was now out of money and worse off than ever. When Jesus came to her town, she pushed through the crowds to see him. "If I but touch his clothes, I will be made well" (5:28). When she did, her bleeding stopped instantly. This remarkable story tells us that sometimes our human efforts at healing are insufficient. Sometimes, only God can heal us.

This belief that medicine is not always the complete answer is gaining acceptance within the medical community itself. An increasing number of doctors are acknowledging a strong, positive relationship between faith and medical healing. Respected researchers espouse a significant link between religious faith and physical healing.

Trust in Jesus

Do you believe in Jesus' desire to heal physically? Remember, he is Almighty God. He has authority over sickness. He is the Lord "who heals all your diseases" (Psalm 103:3). Ask Jesus to help you overcome your doubts. Trust in him and in his promises. Jesus meant it when he said, "Whatever you ask for in prayer, believe that you have received it, and it will be yours" (Mark 11:24). He meant it when he said, "If you do not doubt in your heart, but believe that what you say will come to pass, it will be done for you" (11:23).

Now it's up to you. Begin by asking Jesus to heal a sickness that is afflicting you or someone close to you. Sometimes it is good to "command" the sickness to go away "in the name of Jesus" (Acts 3:6). This takes only a few minutes. Then place your hands upon the sick person and pray—every day if necessary. Pray alone, with members of your family and relatives, or with your community. Invite neighbors over to pray with you, if you think it's appropriate. Even people with little or no faith can join in. Just pray and do not lose heart. Follow the example of Jesus, his first disciples, and the long line of saints and heroes of the faith who have gone before us. In the name of Jesus, may we all know his healing touch!

CHAPTER 11

KEYS TO EFFECTIVE EVANGELIZATION

It was a big evening for St. Nicholas Parish. Members—young and old alike—had gathered for a party to celebrate the parish's seventy-fifth anniversary. As they reminisced about the parish's history, Paul, a member of a parish prayer group, noted how he had grown in the area of evangelization. "At first," he said, "it was something I did out of a sense of duty. But now, it flows more easily. I feel as if I have a more genuine desire to care for the people with whom I share the gospel."

Paul came to know Jesus in a life-changing way through a campus evangelistic group when he was in college. "Everything I had learned about Christianity moved from my mind into my heart. Jesus loved me! I was forgiven! He died for me!"

At first, Paul felt a tremendous obligation to tell everyone he met about Jesus, though he didn't really want to evangelize. "Wherever I was—at a gas station, in line at the grocery store, or sitting next to someone on a bus—I felt as if God was expecting me to preach the gospel. Sometimes I'd even try to lead a person in a prayer to Jesus—all with very little success. I guess I had a lot of growing up to do!"

How many of us can identify with Paul's experience! As Christians, we know we should evangelize, yet we feel an almost instinctive resistance to bringing up a subject that many people consider very personal. But Jesus didn't come to make us feel guilty or to lay an impossible burden on us. He came to fill us with his Spirit, and by the power of that Spirit, we all can become powerful witnesses to Jesus' love and presence.

A Simple Method

The key to evangelism is to pray for people, to care for them, and to share with them from our hearts how Jesus has changed our lives. Let's take a look at each of these elements before we focus on the gospel message we are called to proclaim.

The Power of Intercessory Prayer

How quick we can be to underestimate the power of prayer—the foundation for everything Jesus did when he walked the earth! Jesus prayed at important moments in his life, such as at his baptism and his transfiguration (Luke 3:21-22; 9:29-30). But he also prayed before he preached or healed or taught (Matthew 14:19-20; Mark 1:35-39; John 11:41-44). It seems he always sought his Father's guidance and relied on his Father's power.

When we pray for people, it shouldn't be according to our own agenda for them. Rather, we should pray that God will meet whatever needs they have and draw them closer to him. Mark, a member of the St. Nicholas outreach committee, confessed that he used to pray that God would bring tribulation into the life of his best friend so that in his desperation he would turn to God. As he matured, however, Mark realized that this prayer was more like a curse on his friend than a blessing. He came to see that, rather than being like Jesus, the compassionate Savior, he was more like a harsh judge wreaking havoc on his unbelieving friend.

At its heart, evangelization is about sharing the love of Christ with people. God wants to give us compassion for the needs of our friends, our families, and even strangers. He wants to break down any sense of self-righteousness, judgment, or fear that might keep us from sharing his love. That's why prayer is so vital. When we pray, we open our hearts not only to God, but also to the hurts and the needs of those around us.

The Power of Personal Care

It's been said that the only gospel some people will read is the one written on our hearts. You are Jesus' hands and feet! He calls you to reach out and love people, seeing them with his eyes and hearing them with his ears. Without concrete actions, our attempts at evangelization will bear little fruit. If in prayer the Lord compels us to care for those around us, then our caring will eventually open the door to opportunities to share the love of Jesus with others.

Terri, a lector at St. Nicholas Parish, told how she had developed a friendship with Susan, the mother of her son's best friend. "I would pray for Susan every day and try to be a good neighbor to her. Before long, we were taking walks together and talking about our kids. We really enjoyed each other's company. When Susan became sick and had to be hospitalized last year, it seemed only natural for me to help out. I cooked meals for her family, looked after her children, and visited her. Because we had become friends, it felt natural for me to offer to pray with her for healing. I didn't share my faith with her out of obligation, but because I really like her."

Terri's simple invitation to walk together developed into opportunities to tell Susan about her trust in God and her faith in Jesus' power to heal. As a result, not only did Susan experience some gradual healing, she also opened her heart to Jesus and began attending a women's group in the parish.

The Power of Personal Testimony

What would you say if someone told you that hazelnut chocolates have 25 percent total fat, 1 percent sodium, 6 percent carbohydrates, 4 percent fiber, and four grams of protein? Would these statistics make you want to go out and eat some? Probably not! Similarly, we might explain all the facts about Christianity and still not proclaim the good news. Imagine how different your reaction would be if that person said, "Hey, these hazelnut chocolates taste great! You should try one."

Sharing the gospel is first and foremost telling people about what Jesus has done for us. Sharing our personal experiences of the risen Lord is more likely to capture people's imaginations and rouse their interest than talking about complex theological issues. The fine points of Christian dogma can be left for later discussions. Throughout the Acts of the Apostles, we see the first Christians talking about the risen Jesus as someone they knew and experienced personally. They invited people not to debate doctrine but to experience the Lord for themselves through repentance and conversion of heart.

Like the first Christians, we can share our experience of Jesus and our love for him with those around us. We can speak with an authority that flows from Jesus, an authority that no amount of study can duplicate. Mary, another woman in St. Nicholas Parish, put it this way: "If I let my faith become passive—if I'm not in touch with the Lord in prayer and Scripture—my desire to love people and to share with them melts away. But when I am seeking the presence of God every day, then I love sharing with my friends and neighbors."

We Are Jesus' Hands and Feet

One day, when he was visiting the pool of Siloam—known for its healing powers—Jesus met a man who had been lame for thirty-eight years. "Do you want to be healed?" he asked. The man replied, "Sir, I have no one to put me into the pool" (John 5:6-7). Can you imagine how lonely this man felt? Abandoned, he had no one to take care of him, no one to bring him to the healing he needed, until he met Jesus.

But we are Jesus' body! We are his hands and his feet, his eyes and his ears in this world. So many people are like this lame man. So many cry out in their hearts, "I have no one to heal me. I have no one to tell me that God really loves me." Can we open our hearts to the cries of those who don't know the love of the Father? Can we pray and ask the Holy Spirit to change our hearts as well as theirs? Can we reach out in the love of Christ to care for them and share the good news? Let's ask God to fill us with the compassion, wisdom, and boldness of Christ.

Good News You Can Use

As we mentioned above, when we truly care for other people, we will be moved to pray for them, and ultimately this will open the door to sharing with them the message of Jesus' love. Yet how do we minister to so many different human hearts? St. Paul answered this question by saying, "I have become all things to all people, that I might by all means save some" (1 Corinthians 9:22). In other words, Paul shared those aspects of his life that most closely connected with the experiences or needs of the people to whom he was witnessing. When he preached to Jewish people, he spoke about how Jesus is the fulfillment of the promises God made to Abraham, Moses, and David. When he shared with gentiles, he spoke less about the history of Israel and more about the power of Jesus' resurrection to free people from sin.

In every situation, Paul tried to identify with and meet the needs of his listeners. Similarly, each of the four gospels has a slightly different approach to the way it tells the story of Jesus—each approach based on the needs and character of the community for which it was written. Even Jesus varied his approach. He could be patient and kind toward repentant sinners but firm and confrontational with the self-righteous. How did Jesus know what to say in each situation? He listened to his Father! In much the same way, we are at our best when we ask the Holy Spirit to guide our thoughts, words, and actions.

Though Jesus varied his presentation, the heart of his message was always the same, just as it was for all the early Christians. At its core, effective evangelism always flows from the testimony of a personal encounter with God. On Easter Sunday, Mary Magdalene told the apostles, "I have seen the Lord!" (John 20:18). Addressing a crowd of people not long after Pentecost, Peter said, "We are witnesses to all that [Jesus] did" (Acts 10:39). Near the end of his life, John wrote, "That which we have seen and heard we proclaim also to you" (1 John 1:3). These disciples, and countless Christians in every age, testify to a personal encounter with Jesus. God is real in my life! I have tasted his love, and you can experience him too!

Changed by the Love of God

Many psychologists have observed that no matter how secure and self-confident a person may appear, everyone is anxious and insecure in some way. Regardless of our physical condition, financial situation, or social standing, we all long for a sense of meaning and purpose. We long for a love that is stable, unconditional, and freely given. Although human love is powerful in and of itself, only Jesus can meet all of our needs. This is why St. Augustine wrote, "Our hearts are restless until they rest in you, O Lord."

It seems that everyone has particular times of openness, moments when he or she is able to recognize a personal need for the Lord.

Take St. Augustine as a prime example. Augustine was a brilliant teacher and philosopher who sought truth in pagan religions. His mother, Monica, was a devout Christian who prayed constantly for her son. But as hard as Monica prayed, and as much as she tried to reach Augustine with the gospel, it took years and some very difficult situations before her words could penetrate Augustine's heart and open him to Christ.

In the end, it wasn't Monica's words or her ability to philosophize that changed Augustine. It was her love, her prayer, and the fact that she was always available to him, ready to help him when his time finally came. Her love and concern for Augustine never wavered. As we learn to love people as faithfully as Monica loved Augustine, we too stand a chance of being there when the moment comes for them—the time when they recognize their need for the Lord and his salvation. Then we can share with them the same love of God that has given us such hope and confidence.

A Love That Pardons and Restores

What might we want to say to someone? No single script answers every person's needs. Yet there are some key, central elements to the message of God's love. The following are examples of some of the things we might say as we introduce the gospel message.

"You may find it hard to believe that God could love you so much as to forgive all your sins. I found it hard, too. Deep inside, I would sometimes have a sense of unworthiness, a belief that I didn't deserve to be loved unconditionally, as I was told God loved me. And I was right! None of us deserves such love. But that doesn't matter to God. He loves us anyway. He looks beyond the things we've done and sees us as his children created in his image and likeness."

"I've come to realize that nothing I've done in the past or will do in the future could ever alter God's love for me. It's the same for you, too. His love is so strong that he willingly took on all the sin and darkness in your heart and mine and overcame it with his goodness and holiness. Jesus went so far as to surrender to death on a cross just to remove every obstacle that kept us from him."

"It's taken me a long time, but I've come to realize a little of the immensity of Jesus' love for us. Think about everything he did when he was on the earth: He healed the sick, fed the hungry, forgave sinners, and released those in bondage. Everything he said and did revealed the lengths to which God would go to release us from sin. All he asks of us is the same thing he asked of his listeners two thousand years ago: 'Repent, and believe in the good news' (Mark 1:15). Just as he told a woman caught in sin, he tells us, 'Has no one condemned you? . . . Neither do I condemn you; go, and do not sin again' (John 8:10-11)."

"If you're anything like me, you probably know that some of the things you've done—maybe even some of the things you're doing now—are not pleasing to God. Our sins block us from receiving his love, and this is why Jesus calls us to repentance. He doesn't want us to feel condemned. He wants us to turn to him, accept the forgiveness he won for us, and ask for the power of his Holy Spirit to help us stay faithful to him."

"You know me well enough to know that I'm no saint. I've done some pretty selfish and unloving things at times. But I know that Jesus has already died for the wrongs I've done and the wrongs done to me. His death atoned for every single human transgression. My sin and weakness—and yours as well—may have cut us off from God, but because of Jesus, we can be forgiven and restored."

"In the Book of Jeremiah, God said, 'I know the plans I have for you, plans for welfare and not for evil, to give you a future and a hope' (29:11). God really does have a beautiful plan for our lives. He wants to free us from the things that drag us down. He wants to fill us with his love and lift us up with the knowledge of his promises. All you need to do is pray, read Scripture, and ask Jesus to come into your life."

"It's okay to put Jesus to the test. If he really is the Son of God, then he must be able to reveal himself to you personally. If he really does love you this deeply, how could he not answer your prayer?"

Sharing the Love of Christ

Remember, there is no perfect formula or script. The previous paragraphs speak of God's love, our sin, and the forgiveness available in Jesus. No matter how you get these points across to someone, remember to pray, love, and speak from the heart about your own experience of Christ. God can do a lot with an open heart and a mind docile to the Holy Spirit. Let's all strive to become "all things to all people" in the hope of bringing them to know the love of Christ, which surpasses all knowledge.

CHAPTER 12

FIGHTING TO WIN THE SPIRITUAL BATTLE

Scripture and the saints have consistently described the Christian life in terms of a spiritual battle or spiritual warfare. They explain how good is opposed to evil, right is opposed to wrong, God is opposed to Satan, and heaven is opposed to hell. This image of spiritual warfare can help us identify the ways in which Satan seeks to influence us and turn us against what is good and what is of God.

If we take our faith personally, we will often find ourselves engaged in some kind of spiritual struggle. The closer we draw to God, the more Satan will want to tear us away. So what strategies can help us fight and win these battles? What defensive and offensive tools does Scripture tell us to use? Then what is the prize for winning the spiritual battle; what are we fighting for?

Strategies for Winning against the Enemy

The mind is God's most precious gift to us. It is capable of reasoning, imagining, expressing and receiving affection, making decisions, and committing things to memory. The mind is also the place of conscience—that unique human ability to choose right from wrong. God wants us to use our minds to love him and one another.

He wants us to use our wills, our intellects, and our imaginations to share the gospel, to feed the hungry, and to bring his justice into this world.

But God hasn't left us to work all this out on our own. He wants to transform our minds through the power of his grace. He wants to reveal his intentions to us and give us his wisdom. St. Paul goes so far as to say that those who have received the Holy Spirit are able to understand the wisdom of God because they have the very "mind of Christ" (1 Corinthians 2:7, 16).

All this sounds so promising, but Satan has a different goal. He wants to separate us from God and from one another. Satan uses lies, accusations, greed, lust, and a host of other tactics to tempt us and lead us into sin. He wants to see our sins separate us from God and dull our consciences so that we will sin more freely. Then, when our consciences do rise up, he whispers words of guilt to convince us that we are beyond hope and that God can never forgive us. As a result of all this guilt and shame, we feel bound up, burdened, and hopelessly distant from God's forgiveness and love.

The Perils of a Mind Filled with Lies

Once we entertain a lie from Satan and allow this lie to influence our actions, new lies reinforce and build upon the initial lie. After a while, our judgment is confused and unreliable. We find it hard to discern right from wrong, or the ways of God from the ways of Satan. We mistakenly assume sinful behavior to be right—even though this behavior is clearly opposed to God's commands.

King David is one example of this cycle of lies leading to greater sin. David was attracted to and slept with Bathsheba, the wife of Uriah (2 Samuel 11:2-4). In committing this act of adultery, both David and Bathsheba sinned against God.

This is how the story looked on the human level. But behind the scenes, Satan was at work as well. Through his own seductive temptations, he was encouraging this whole sinful encounter. And then? The lies from Satan only increased. He convinced David to cover up his sin by trying to deceive Uriah and ultimately kill him. It took a confrontation from the prophet Nathan to open David's eyes to all his wrongdoing. Finally, David repented and reestablished his relationship with God.

This biblical story shows that Satan's lures can lead us to make decisions that we know are opposed to God's commands. It shows that we can silence our consciences and somehow believe that actions clearly opposed to God's commands are acceptable. Had David been on the alert, he could have seen the temptation for what it was and chosen to walk away. Finally, this story shows that our God is always willing to show us mercy. No sin, not even adultery or murder, is outside of his power to forgive.

Winning the Battle for the Mind

Satan will use any means to defeat us. He will whisper words of low self-esteem or high self-esteem. He will try to weigh us down with guilt or dull our consciences. He will try to move us to lash out in anger or convince us to keep all our emotions bottled up. He will try any strategy to keep us from using our minds for God's glory and to convince us to make selfish choices opposed to God's plans. And as a result, we will find ourselves hurting others and being separated from God.

So what can we do to win this battle for the mind? Let's consider a few strategies.

Build a Godly Database

One of the most effective weapons we have in the spiritual battle is what St. Paul called the "belt of truth" (Ephesians 6:14). David's eyes were opened as Nathan spoke the "truths" of God to him, and the same can happen to us. We will be able to choose God and reject Satan only if we know who God is—if we know about his love, his many attributes, and his glorious plan for all humanity. Here is a brief list of just a few basic truths we should never let out of our minds:

(1) God loves me (see Romans 8:38-39; 1 John 4:10).
(2) God has a perfect plan for me (see Jeremiah 29:11; Psalm 139:3, 16).
(3) Jesus has forgiven all sin (see Mark 10:45; 1 John 2:1-2).
(4) I am a new creation in Christ (see Romans 6:4; 2 Corinthians 5:17).
(5) Jesus has defeated the devil (see John 12:31-32; Colossians 1:13-14).
(6) The Holy Spirit lives in me (see Luke 11:13; Romans 8:15-16).

(7) I can overcome evil with good (see Matthew 5:14-16; Ephesians 5:8-11).

Know That You Are a Child of God

Equally important as building a godly database, we need to discover our true identity as children of God. Satan lies. He tells us that we do not have a loving Father in heaven. He tries to hide our everlasting heritage from us. He downplays what Jesus did for us on the cross and tells us instead that we are equal to God and that we don't need God. Let's not be like the child who goes through life completely unaware that his father has left him a million-dollar inheritance. Rather, let's claim this glorious promise that is part of our inheritance in Christ.

Take Your Thoughts Captive

On a practical level, St. Paul tells us to "take every thought captive to obey Christ" (2 Corinthians 10:5). When our minds are grounded in the truth—about who God is and who we are as his children—we will be better able to counteract the lies of Satan. With this protective foundation of truth in place, we can then take hold of our thoughts and discern whether they are in line with the Lord.

And this is not just a human exercise we are meant to go through. As we try to take our thoughts captive, we will find the Holy Spirit helping us to determine whether they are consistent with the gospel and whether they will help us fulfill our desire to be obedient to

Christ. St. Paul gave us the right way to live for God: "Whatever is true, whatever is honorable, whatever is just, whatever is pure, whatever is pleasing, whatever is commendable, if there is any excellence and if there is anything worthy of praise, think about these things" (Philippians 4:8).

God Is with Us

Brothers and sisters, God wants to help us win the battle. With this truth firmly planted in our minds, we don't have to be anxious about anything. Instead, in every situation, using "prayer and supplication with thanksgiving," we can tell God what we need. Then God's own peace, "which surpasses all understanding, will guard your hearts and your minds in Christ Jesus" (Philippians 4:6-7).

God has given us the Holy Spirit. He has given us the body and blood of his Son in the Eucharist. These are tremendous provisions, which can help us overcome the lies of the devil. Winning the battle for our minds is not an easy task. Yet there is nothing more gratifying and more pleasing to God than our victory over Satan. After all, God created us to be free (Galatians 5:1)!

Wearing the Armor of God

Be strong in the Lord and in the strength of his might. Put on the whole armor of God, that you may be able to stand against the wiles of the devil. For we are not contending against flesh and blood, but against the principalities, against the powers, against the world rulers of this present darkness, against the spiritual hosts of wickedness in the heavenly places. (Ephesians 6:10-12)

What's the goal of your faith? To believe in the truths of the Nicene Creed and attend Sunday Mass? To do good works of service or ministry? To put the majority of your energy into your work, your ministry, or your family?

Faith in the creed, service to others, working hard, caring for loved ones, and trying to have a pure disposition are, to be sure, important dimensions in our lives. Yet these virtues are not the primary tools St. Paul describes as the "armor of God." According to Paul, these approaches will not necessarily give us the wisdom and power we need to "stand up against the wiles of the devil."

A Roman Analogy

Paul's catchy phrase, "the full armor of God," comes from his own experience. Both as a Roman citizen and later as a prisoner under Roman guard, Paul had become familiar with the soldiers of Rome. He regularly saw them in their military outfits—helmets, breastplates, belts, foot guards, shields—all meant to protect them from enemy attack. He knew that the relatively smaller and lighter swords they used gave them a competitive advantage over other soldiers, who had longer, heavier swords. He knew about the Roman "platoon," a small, decentralized group of soldiers who could respond quickly to a number of military situations. He knew that Rome had conquered most of the world in part because they had developed one of the best-trained armies of ancient history.

Paul took this military imagery—which was also familiar to most of his readers—and applied it to the Christian life as a way of teaching how to fight against the lies of Satan. He wanted believers to learn how to hold their spiritual ground. For Paul, this meant they needed to protect their eyes, ears, minds, and hearts.

In Paul's mind, people needed a balance between the normal demands and joys of everyday life—such as education, personal development, work, family, health, and finances—and the spiritual dimension of life, which was focused on experiencing fellowship with God. In his own experience and through observing others, Paul saw the correlation between putting on the armor of God and being able to recognize and resist Satan's deceptions. Those who did not take such a stand were far more vulnerable to Satan. Those who gave in to the devil's lies became further separated from God, forgot what it was like to experience his love, and lost sight of God's desire to transform them into his sons and his daughters.

Images of the Armor of God

In writing about the armor of God, Paul gave his readers the remedy for standing firm and implored them to use this armor to defend themselves against Satan. He told them to buckle the "belt of truth" around their waists (Isaiah 11:5); to put on the "breastplate of righ-teousness" (59:17); to have their feet fitted with the "gospel of peace" (52:7); to put on the "shield of faith" (Psalm 28:7) and the "helmet of salvation" (Isaiah 59:17); and, finally, to take up the "sword of the Spirit, which is the word of God" (Isaiah 49:2).

Of these six images, five refer to defensive armor; only one—the sword of the Spirit—is an offensive weapon. Paul understood that a sound Christian character grounded in truth, honesty, and integrity is the first line of spiritual defense. The second line is our experience of the grace and peace of God at work. And the final line of defense is our ability to wield the word of God like a two-edged sword, sharpening our convictions about Christ and cutting away all the empty rhetoric Satan uses to dull our minds and lead us into temptation.

Through Christ, God has given us everything we need to fight the good fight and win the battle for our minds. Our ability to stand firm in this battle depends in part upon our own resolve to fight against Satan. But our human efforts are not enough. An even greater element in our strategy must be our reliance upon the grace and power of the Holy Spirit.

We *can* be strong in the Lord. We can put on God's armor and stand up against the lies of Satan. The question becomes, "Why go through such a strenuous effort? Is it really necessary?" And the answer for anyone who wants to know God's presence is a resounding yes. If you want intimacy with God, if knowing God's love is critical for your life, then you can have it—if you are willing to persevere and take your stand against the spiritual forces of evil.

Motivated by Love

Of all the goals and plans God has for his creation, his first priority has always been to bring every human being to him. God wants to see everyone "confess and believe" that his Son, Jesus Christ, is Savior and Lord (Romans 10:9). He wants to see everyone go to heaven. Beyond this first goal of salvation, however, our heavenly Father wants to have a loving relationship with us. He wants all of us to know his blessings and his intimate love. So let's take a look at this prize of intimacy with God so that we can be even more motivated to take up the battle and persist until we see victory.

Knowledge and Experience

From experience, St. Paul knew that there was a correlation among our knowledge of God's truths, our experience of God's love, and our willingness to stand firm. He knew that when truth and experience were both active in a person's life it would be much easier to stand firm against the devil's wiles.

When a man gets married, he promises to be devoted to his wife. This promise calls him to "stand firm" and say no to wandering eyes and wandering thoughts. When this truth is muddled, and he lets his eyes and thoughts wander, temptation has won some ground in him—and it may win more ground. Clearly, there is a strong correlation between the man's grasp of the temptations he faces, his decision to stand firm against them, and his ability to share love with his wife.

In the same way, our intimacy with God is closely linked to—dare we say, the driving force behind—our decision to take up the battle for our minds. The experience of God's love in our hearts drives us to fight against anything that seeks to rob us of intimacy with God.

An Open-and-Shut Case

When Paul first visited Ephesus, he found a group of people who had been disciples of John the Baptist. When he asked them, "Did you receive the Holy Spirit when you believed?" they said, "No, we have never even heard that there is a Holy Spirit" (Acts 19:2). Paul told them that the baptism of Jesus—which they had yet to receive—was different from John's. The baptism of Jesus was not limited to repentance, but included the power of the Holy Spirit to bring believers into union with God. These Ephesian disciples eagerly accepted this baptism; when Paul laid his hands on them and prayed, "they all were filled with the Holy Spirit" (19:3-6).

If we want to have intimacy with God, it starts with the Holy Spirit. This is one of the clearest truths in the Bible. Paul repeatedly challenged his readers to seek the Holy Spirit. He urged the Romans to live in accord with the Spirit (Romans 8:4, 11). He urged the Corinthians to seek the wisdom of God through the Spirit and to use the gifts of the Spirit (1 Corinthians 2:10; 12:7-11). He told the Thessalonians, "our gospel came to you not only in word, but also in power and in the Holy Spirit and with full conviction" (1 Thessalonians 1:5).

God wants intimacy with us. He wants to draw us into his presence and fill us to overflowing with his love. However, we can't be passive bystanders. If we take our faith seriously, it's up to us to listen for the voice of the Holy Spirit. It's up to us to open the door of our hearts when we hear God knocking. It's also up to us to "bolt" the door of our minds when we hear the voice of the liar. His only goal is to convince us to turn away from Jesus and ask Jesus to get out of our lives. This is why as Spirit-filled Catholics who are being transformed by our faith, we need to take a stand against Satan's schemes. We need to ask the Holy Spirit to come into our hearts and lovingly lead us—and the whole church—to Jesus.

CHAPTER 13

THE POWER OF INTERCESSORY PRAYER

There are many ways to love one's neighbor, but intercessory prayer—praying on behalf of other people—has got to be one of the most powerful. Prayer is the most potent force known to humanity. Because we have been made partakers in Jesus' victory over sin and death (1 John 4:4), we have the authority as sons and daughters of God to pray for others, pushing back the darkness of sin and oppression. In prayer, we have a weapon that has "divine power to destroy strongholds" (2 Corinthians 10:4).

That kind of weaponry—the power of prayer—is something God invites us to use as we seek not only personal transformation but the transformation of the world as well. In this chapter, we'll take a look at some lessons we can learn about intercession from the witness of one Old Testament prophet. Then, we'll see what we can learn from Jesus' own prayer life. And finally we'll look at the authority we have as intercessors here and now.

As you read this chapter, ask the Spirit to teach you how to pray in union with the mind of God. Take to heart St. Paul's words, "The Spirit helps us in our weakness; for we do not know how to pray as we ought, but that very Spirit intercedes . . . for the saints according to the will of God" (Romans 8:26-27). And above all, ask God to give you confidence that he hears your prayers and longs to answer the deep needs of those around you.

The Example of Biblical Intercessors

The Old Testament provides powerful portraits of intercessors whose example can teach and encourage us. Rather than just tell God all that they wanted to see happen in the world, these intercessors sought first and foremost to understand *his* mind and *his* will. They waited upon the Spirit and pondered God's word until they knew *how* to pray and *what* to pray for.

These heroes and heroines of Israel placed more confidence in God's words to them than in their own opinions or the opinions of others. They humbly sought to obey God, even in the face of ridicule and opposition. Let's take for our example the prophet Habakkuk.

Habakkuk: Praying the Mind of God

The Book of Habakkuk provides a powerful and clear portrait of someone who learned how to intercede. The book is short enough to be read in one sitting, which is probably also the best way to understand Habakkuk's intercession.

Taking Up a "Burden"

The very first verse shows us that an intercessor is one who takes up a "burden" that goes far beyond his or her own needs and intentions. Habakkuk lived between the late seventh and early sixth centuries before Christ, a time of spiritual, moral, and political decline for Jerusalem. He was deeply wounded in conscience by the violence and oppression that surrounded him—his fellow Israelites seemed to have total disregard for the Lord and his commandments. In grief over his people's condition, Habakkuk cried out to the Lord.

Habakkuk felt free enough to complain to God, but he was also careful not to tell him what to do. How often do we recognize a problem and then immediately ask God to solve that problem in a certain way? God wants us to become intercessors like Habakkuk. After talking to God about the problem, he waited for God to answer and was willing to hear even an answer he wouldn't like.

And God did answer. He told Habakkuk that, rather than rescuing Jerusalem, he was raising up the Babylonians to enact his judgment: "I am rousing the Chaldeans, that bitter and hasty nation, who march through the breadth of the earth, to seize habitations not their own" (1:6).

Astonished, Habakkuk acknowledged that God had every right to do as he said he would. But Habakkuk nevertheless poured out a second complaint. *Lord, how could such a wicked nation be sent against your people?* He then took up a position of prayer and watchfulness until he heard an answer. Like a humble but persistent soldier, he was willing to wrestle in prayer, deep into the night, if necessary, to get his answer. "I will take my stand to watch, and station myself on the tower, and look forth to see what he will say to me, and what I will answer concerning my complaint" (2:1).

A Union of Wills

Eventually, Habakkuk received his reply. God told him to write down the revelation and publicize it throughout the kingdom. In doing so, Habakkuk became a spiritual father to the people of Jerusalem, offering prophetic words of warning and encouragement to God's children.

What was the answer Habakkuk received? "He whose soul is not upright in him shall fail, but the righteous shall live by his faith" (2:4). Habakkuk saw that his people were about to experience the catastrophe of enemy occupation, the destruction of their temple, and exile. God was bringing his people into a situation so traumatic that they would not be able to think, manipulate, or bully their way out of it. They would be humbled to such a degree that their only recourse would be faith—trust in God and obedience to the law that they had abandoned. They would come to learn that Yahweh, their God, was always near to those who called upon him. They would also learn that, even in the midst of judgment from the Lord, God works all things for the good of those who love him (Romans 8:28; Hebrews 12:5-11).

Sharing in God's Suffering and Hope

Those who take up the call to intercession come to learn that the sufferings of the present time cannot compare to the joy that will come as God's purposes unfold. They learn to trust in the Lord, because they have experienced in prayer how infinitely compassionate God is—he is the deepest sufferer in the universe! Intercessors gain a privileged insight into God's magnificent plan to raise humanity to share in divine life. This insight moves them to engage in a spiritual battle against the forces that seek to destroy God's plans.

The final chapter of the Book of Habakkuk gives us a glimpse into the heart of an intercessor—both in his praying for a mighty outpouring of grace, and in his abandonment and trust in God's provision. Let us take Habakkuk's prayer as our own as we intercede for the many needs of the church and the world: "O LORD, I have heard of your renown, and I stand in awe, O LORD, of your work. In our own time revive it; in our own time make it known; in wrath may you remember mercy" (3:2).

Jesus: The Most Powerful Intercessor

The Letter of James tells us that "The prayer of a righteous man has great power in its effects" (James 5:16), and there is no one more righteous than Jesus—the most powerful intercessor who ever walked the earth. Martha, sister to Lazarus, rightly declared, "Lord, if you had been here, my brother would not have died. And even now I know that whatever you ask from God, God will give you" (John 11:21-22).

It is amazing to consider that every prayer that Jesus ever made was answered. It is even more amazing to learn that Jesus wants to make us into powerful intercessors, as well—men and women of faith who receive whatever we ask for (John 14:12-14). Let's take a look at Jesus' teaching and prayer so that by his word and example we can learn to pray effectively.

When teaching his disciples to pray, Jesus told them to call God "Father" (Matthew 6:9-13). How easy it is to memorize the Our Father and yet miss out on all the depth contained in it! When we pray the Our Father for other people, do we think about what we are saying? Do we seek to actually live out the words we are praying?

Moved by God's Love

The first three petitions in the Our Father are that the name of God would be honored and held sacred, that his kingdom would come about, and that his will would be accomplished on earth as perfectly as it is in heaven.

Throughout his life, Jesus not only prayed this prayer, he fulfilled it. He was so moved by the generosity and expansiveness of his Father's love that he constantly prayed that people would embrace the life his Father offered and commit themselves to advancing his kingdom on earth. This was no half-hearted recitation of requests, but a prayer in faith, trusting that God would hear him and enable him to fulfill the task he was sent to accomplish.

Throughout his life, Jesus received whatever he asked for in prayer. Just think about how perfectly he loved and honored God. Both by his perfect obedience and by the victory of his resurrection, Jesus has hallowed and brought glory to his Father's name (John 17:1-2).

By his preaching, his miracles, and most important, his cross, he has established the kingdom of God on earth. He has undone the works of the devil and destroyed the power of sin that held us in bondage. As citizens of the kingdom of God, we can now advance this kingdom in the world as we deepen our relationship with him and receive his Spirit's power to reflect God's justice and mercy (John 17:3).

Jesus' commitment to the prayer that God's will be done was vividly evident in the garden of Gethsemane, when he prayed, "My Father, if it be possible, let this cup pass from me; yet not what I want but what you want" (Matthew 26:39). His obedience to the Father's will ushered in the kingdom he so longed for.

This greatest of intercessors was consumed with the desire to love and obey his Father. It is, in fact, this love Jesus has for God that moves him to love us as deeply as he does. He wants to heal us, deliver us, and give us abundant life here and now. Even more important, he wants to make us one with the Father and draw us into eternal life with him in heaven.

Moved to Love Others

While the first three petitions of the Our Father have to do with our God, the last four have to do with us, his people. Jesus told his disciples to pray for daily bread, for forgiveness, for divine guidance, and for deliverance from evil.

Again we can see how perfectly Jesus lived out these prayers. In the miracle of the loaves and fishes, Jesus showed that he cares for our practical needs. But this miracle also shows that Jesus goes even further to provide us with the bread of his word and with his very body in the Eucharist.

His commitment to forgiveness is evident in his prayer from the cross: "Father, forgive them; for they know not what they do" (Luke 23:34).

And he earnestly prayed for the two men crucified with him, that in their final hour they would not succumb to temptation! We see the fruit of this intercession in the conversion of one of these men and in Jesus' promise that he would be with him in paradise (Luke 23:39-43).

Finally, Jesus not only delivered people tormented by evil spirits, he also prayed for our protection from evil: "Simon, Simon, behold, Satan demanded to have you, that he might sift you like wheat, but I have prayed for you that your faith may not fail" (Luke 22:31-32). "I do not pray that you take them out of the world, but that you keep them from the evil one" (John 17:15).

The Heart of Intercession: Union with God

There is so much more that we could say about Jesus' prayer to the Father and his intercession for us. He is our great high priest; he never stops presenting himself to the Father as our advocate; his heart is always on fire with love for his bride, the church.

Take some time to ponder the Our Father and how perfectly Jesus lived out this prayer. Open your heart to the Lord and ask him to show you how everything Jesus prayed—everything he did—was so that we might learn to call God our Father. God wants us to know our dignity as his beloved children. We can turn to him at any point in our day and talk to him about our needs and the needs of those around us. We can live as Jesus did, in reverent submission to the Father, knowing the great blessings of being in his presence.

Jesus wants to take us beyond just praying for other people. He wants to form us into his own image. At the heart of all intercession is taking on Jesus' character to the point where we rejoice with him over the repentance of one sinner (Luke 15:7) and weep with him over those who have yet to embrace him and his word (19:41-42; Philippians 3:18-19). Let's ask God to teach us the inner life of Jesus—not just his words, but his thoughts, desires, and intentions.

From all eternity, Jesus is praying for you and calling you into perfect union with him. Yes, we will share in his sufferings, but we will also share in his perfect peace, perfect joy, and the perfect love that casts out fear. We will also see his perfect power released in and through us in an ever-increasing way.

Powerful and Effective: Our Authority as Intercessors

The Letter to the Hebrews tells us that because Jesus' priesthood is eternal, "he is able for all time to save those who draw near to God through him, since he always lives to make intercession for them" (7:25). Imagine that: right now, Jesus is in heaven interceding for you, even as he intercedes for the entire world. He also invites us all to join in his priestly intercession so that a mighty flood of prayer will ascend to the Father's throne.

Prayer Makes a Difference

Let us not be deceived: the devil wants to convince us that our prayer accomplishes nothing. But history has consistently proven him wrong. When Mary, the mother of God, appeared to three simple peasant children in Fatima in 1917, she taught them how to intercede, and the results were remarkable. Mary warned these children that although the current war would soon end, an even worse war would come if people did not repent. She also warned against errors coming from Russia that would wreak havoc on the church and the world.

To avert these disasters, Mary asked the children to urge all the church to repent and pray for the conversion of Russia. At that time, no one thought Russia—a relatively backward country undergoing political upheaval—would have much impact on the world scene. Those who took up Mary's message were ridiculed. Of course within twenty years, the world was plunged into another major war. But then the prophetic message of Fatima was taken more seriously. Like Habakkuk, many people took up a position of watchful prayer, waiting for the Lord to act (see Habakkuk 2:1). Finally, in the late 1980s, Communism in Russia and throughout Eastern Europe collapsed with surprisingly less bloodshed than was feared. The legions of intercessors changed the course of history!

Two Kinds of Wisdom

Do you want to rely only on your limited human wisdom to determine what you should ask for in prayer? It is good to pray according to the needs we perceive, but joining Jesus in intercession requires that we also ask the Spirit to reveal how he wants us to pray. It requires that we ask him to place a burden upon our hearts to see God's desires fulfilled. When we bend ourselves to God in this way, we open our hearts to his grace and revelation, for at the core of all intercession is the Holy Spirit, praying for the church.

How wonderful to experience the Holy Spirit uniting us with Jesus as he intercedes for his people! What a privilege to stand cleansed in the living water of the triune God—a mystery described as being in the midst of three blissful rivers unceasingly emptying into each other.

As we are raised in Christ Jesus beyond the limits of our natural minds, our prayer will be lifted higher. For example, a simple analysis of good and evil may lead us to pray for pro-life legislation, but it may not cause us to understand why people would consider killing their unborn children. We need God's word to reveal to us the root causes of such desperate actions so that we know more specifically how to pray and act. It is important to change the laws of the land, but it is even more important to change hearts with the gospel. The Lord is concerned with the law, but he is even more concerned for you and for every other individual, for there will be no peace between us until there is peace within us.

A Call for Warriors

Intercessors know that God's people mature as they overcome trials, temptations, and tribulations. Ever since the fall of humanity, life on earth has been subject to the evil one, personal sin, and structures of sin and darkness within society. Even nations in which the majority of people are baptized are not immune. Baptism may have cleansed us from original sin, but we still must deal with the effects of that sin. We may be cleansed, but we do not automatically receive a renewed mind. Scripture cautions us: "If we say we have no sin, we deceive ourselves, and the truth is not in us" (1 John 1:8).

We can either deny the reality of evil or freely choose to turn our lives over to God, who alone can rescue us. Those who put their trust in riches, human security, and human power will fall short. So too will those who trust in knowledge or their own self-righteousness. Those who seek escape by abusing alcohol, sex, or drugs may find temporary relief, but in the long run, they will inherit only more pain and isolation. Again, Scripture warns that the world is under the control of the "evil one" (1 John 5:19). We are in a battle for life. But thanks be to God that we have the victory in Jesus Christ. "Who is it that overcomes the world but he who believes that Jesus is the Son of God?" (5:5).

Jesus told his disciples to pray to the Lord of the harvest to send out laborers into his field (Matthew 9:38). Let us pray and let us labor. Let us feed the hungry, clothe the naked, visit the sick and imprisoned, be kind to strangers, and minister the gospel. But let us also pray without ceasing (1 Thessalonians 5:17).

Tips for Intercessory Prayer

Jesus promised: "If two of you agree on earth about anything they ask, it will be done for them by my Father in heaven" (Matthew 18:19). One of the most powerful ways we can pray as intercessors is together with others. Consider forming an intercessory prayer team. Here are some suggestions that may help:

1. Since it is the prayer of the righteous that is powerful and effective (James 5:16), examine your consciences before you pray, and repent of any sin or harsh feelings you may have against other people.

2. Spend a few minutes in silence, allowing the people in the group to quiet their minds and come into God's presence.

3. During this time, let each person ask the Lord to give him or her a sense of the things God wants each to pray for. Put aside your own agenda, concerns, and desires and unite yourself to Jesus' heart. You may want to write down the things that God places on your hearts.

4. Briefly tell each other what you wrote down. What do you think God is leading your group to pray for? Give special weight to issues that more than one person mentioned.

5. Pray for the things on God's heart—for those who have no faith; for those who have fallen away from Jesus; for renewal and unity in all the Christian churches; for all the lost, abandoned, or forgotten children of the world; for those under the power of addictions or bound by depression, anxiety, or bitterness. Note also the admonition, "The intercession of Christians recognizes no boundaries: 'for all men, for kings and all who are in high positions,' for persecutors, for the salvation of those who reject the Gospel (1 Timothy 2:1; Romans 12:14; 10:1)" (*Catechism of the Catholic Church*, 2636).

6. As you pray, take confidence in God's power to overcome any obstacle. Stand firm in faith, and wait to see God work in power.

7. Keep a record of what you prayed for, and of the ways God answered those prayers. Thank him and praise him for all the ways he has worked through your prayer.

CHAPTER 14

EARTHLY TREASURE, HEAVENLY TREASURE

When we give our lives to Jesus, we give him everything we are and everything we have: our minds, our bodies, our time, our affections, our families. We acknowledge that it's all on "loan" to us, that it all belongs to him. When he walked the earth, Jesus had much to say about stewardship—how we use and manage the goods he gives us. As we grow in our relationship with the Lord, we become more conscious of how we use our money. Are we being generous? Are we caring for the poor? Are we developing and using our talents to support our families and to give glory to God by building his kingdom on earth?

Growing closer to the Lord also makes us aware of how much Jesus wants us to use our material possessions to store up heavenly treasures, not earthly ones (Matthew 6:20). In this chapter, let's consider what Jesus said about money and how he calls us to use our gifts to further his kingdom.

What Does It Mean to Be Generous?

One day during his last week in Jerusalem, Jesus sat down in the Temple court with his disciples to rest. As he surveyed the crowd, he saw many people lined up to offer their Temple tithe. There, amidst wealthy people giving large sums of money, Jesus noticed an older woman dressed in widow's clothing offering her own gift: "two copper coins, which are worth a penny" (Mark 12:42). Struck by this woman's poverty yet love for the Lord, Jesus told his disciples that she had given more than anyone else. "For all of them have contributed out of their abundance; but she out of her poverty has put in everything she had, all she had to live on" (12:44).

Why This Widow?

It is difficult for us to understand the plight of many widows in ancient Israel. When a Jewish man died, his entire inheritance passed to his oldest son, leaving his widow dependent upon her child's generosity. Although the son might be expected to give his mother a small portion of the inheritance, it didn't always happen. Consequently, widows could be left destitute.

In Jesus' day, many poor, devout widows must have frequented the temple. Why did this woman impress Jesus so much? Her clothes probably revealed how poor she was, but it wasn't just her poverty that moved Jesus. Looking into her heart, he saw something that set her apart—an extravagant love for God that demonstrated itself in generosity. This widow lived in oppressive poverty, and yet she didn't blame God for her situation. She did not lose herself in bitterness or despair. Instead, she trusted enough in God's loving care to give him her last penny.

What's more, she wasn't embarrassed by her state. Her faith and trust in God were stronger than any sense of inferiority she may have felt as she stood next to the wealthy. Even though she probably had to beg for her next meal, her one goal at that moment was to give her all to God. When she presented those two precious coins, Jesus saw humility and reliance upon God for everything, even her survival.

Sacrificial Giving

Our love for God should be reflected in our generosity toward him and his people, just as the widow demonstrated her love by her offering. The gift of two copper coins revealed the priorities of her heart: She loved God and she loved the Temple in which he dwelt. Similarly, the way we spend our money reveals our priorities and love.

Over the past decade, scandals in different churches and charitable organizations have caused many Christians to shy away from the call to give generously. But Scripture teaches that it is an honor and a privilege to participate in the building-up of the kingdom of God. In the Old Testament, God's people were commanded to offer 10 percent of all their goods and income. Some New Testament communities went even further. In Jerusalem, for example, the first Christians pooled all of their goods together so that everyone was cared for.

How can we expect the gospel to be proclaimed without our help? As he did in the early church, today God calls us to a sacrificial generosity on behalf of our pastors and our parishes. Imagine what your pastor could do if everyone's sacrifice reflected the poor widow's heart of love. Our generous love for the Lord and his church could minister the gospel to thousands.

The need is great. God knows the needs of your parish perfectly. The closer you get to Jesus' heart, the more the Holy Spirit will show you how he wants you to imitate this humble widow's sacrifice. Ask him to guide you. Mark's story is not intended as a command to give away our last penny and live in poverty. We need to be responsible in our giving. Having said that, responsibility should not cloud God's call to be generous. When we give to God's people, we are giving to Jesus himself.

Giving from Our Poverty

St. Mark's lesson is not just a story of generosity. Jesus was struck by the difference between so many of the wealthy people, who gave from their abundance, and this woman, who gave out of her poverty. She knew that she didn't have to give her last coins to obtain God's love. She already knew he loved her. Neither did her money help much in meeting the financial needs of the Temple. But that wasn't the point either. She gave generously because she loved God.

Like the widow, we are all poor in different ways. Maybe you find it hard to love people outside (or even inside) your family. Yet God asks whether you can share the bit of love you do have with those who need it. Maybe you are devoid of the power to forgive. Can you tell Jesus that you will give what little mercy you have to someone who has hurt you? You may feel that you have no time because your life is so busy. Can you give just a few minutes each day to love Jesus in prayer?

God wants us to know that every gift we give—every sacrifice we make—is noticed and rewarded. His Spirit is always hovering over us, ready to respond to our generosity with an even more generous outpouring of divine love and providence. Let's give our two copper coins to God.

Caring for the Poor

Throughout his ministry, Jesus dedicated himself to reversing the tide of sin in the world. He fed the hungry. He healed the sick. He delivered people from demonic oppression. He inspired the rich to give generously to the poor. He preached good news and filled people with hope. Yet despite all his good works, Jesus told his disciples, "The poor you always have with you" (John 12:8).

Jesus did not change the structure of society or the lot of the poor during his brief life. He knew that poverty could not be solved by human effort alone. Jesus came first and foremost to deal with the root of the problem, which is sin. He came to change our hearts so that we might be empowered to love as purely as he loves. And that is precisely why he died on the cross for us. He knew that there would be no heaven on earth until the sin within us was put to death.

The Power to Love

In every generation, poverty has stood as the most pervasive sign of man's inhumanity to man. Today we the baptized are called to share in Jesus' ministry to a world afflicted by sin. God calls each of us to take hold of the grace he has poured upon us to "preach good news to the poor. . . . To proclaim release to the captives . . . to set at liberty those who are oppressed, to proclaim the acceptable year of the Lord" (Luke 4:18-19).

As the cross of Christ pervades our lives more deeply, we will find ourselves able to love the poor in the power of the Holy Spirit. One of the best-known examples of this principle is Blessed Mother Teresa of Calcutta. Many humanitarians who don't believe in Jesus serve the poor with great compassion. But there was a profound difference in the way Mother Teresa ministered to the unloved. With the eyes of faith, she was able to see Jesus himself in the distressing disguise of the poor. When they looked into her eyes, those for whom she cared also saw Jesus ministering to them through her. This wonderful holiness enabled Mother Teresa to minister to their souls as well as their bodies.

Answering the Cry of the Poor

Not all of us are called to devote our lives to serving the poor as radically as Mother Teresa. But we all have an obligation to care for the needy in our midst. God loves the poor, and he calls us to be his hands and his feet in ministering his love to them. He treasures the special love that many poor people have for him (Luke 21:3). He always hears the cry of the poor (Psalm 34:6, 18).

Most of us are comparatively rich. Because we have received much, much is expected of us (Luke 12:48). Are you aware of the suffering of the poor around the world—the homeless; those displaced by war or famine; the widows, orphans, and invalids who have no one to provide for them; the runaways and castaways who live on city streets? They are all beloved children of God crying out for someone to share his love and provision with them.

The New Testament exhorts us "not to be haughty, nor to set [our] hopes on uncertain riches but on God who richly furnishes us with everything. [We are] to be rich in good deeds . . . and generous, thus laying up for [ourselves] a good foundation for the future" (1 Timothy 6:17-19). It is important that we fund missions that care for the soul as well as the body. When he walked the earth, Jesus' first priority was always to save souls. Therefore, in imitation of our Master, our love and care for the poor—and the charities that we support—should not stop short of preaching the gospel.

God is calling us to be a part of his answer to the cry of the poor as we allow the Holy Spirit to fill us with his generous love. The church has done—and continues to do—some marvelous work on behalf of the needy. Your parish likely has outreach programs designed to minister to the poor. Pray about how God may be calling you to help. You can make a greater difference than you imagine.

A "Poverty of Love"

Mother Teresa understood that the great poverty in the Western world is not so much a poverty of food as it is a poverty of love. People are starving for love, even in our own homes. The Holy Spirit can open our eyes to help us see Christ in these needy ones. The love of God can move us to love even those whose condition might normally repel us.

Jesus Christ is in the poor, the sick, the lonely, and the imprisoned. Let us allow the Spirit in us to reach out and love them. The next time you see a homeless person, don't just give money. Try to see Christ in that person and share the love of God through things as simple as eye contact, a smile, and kind words. Let the love of God flow through you.

The Good and the Bad about Money

In the Sermon on the Mount, Jesus gave us three words of warning related to money. In addition to telling us to be careful not to store up treasures on earth, he warned us not to allow money to dominate our lives and not to worry about our financial needs (Matthew 6:19, 24, 25-31).

But it would be a mistake to think that money is bad in the eyes of the Lord. Money has a good side as well. It can actually enhance our relationship with God as we use it to care for the poor, to help evangelistic efforts, and to bless our friends with acts of generosity. Remember, it is our love of money that is at the root of evil and separates us from God—not money in and of itself (1 Timothy 6:10).

Based on these teachings, we can come to three conclusions: First, God has given us the right to earn a living wage as we develop the talents he has given us. Second, we should be prudent in the way we use and save the money we earn. Third, we should be generous and give as much as we can to others who are in need.

Developing Our Talents

God has given all of us talents, and he expects us to develop these talents in a way that gives him glory and honor. He wants us to use our abilities to provide for ourselves and our families and to contribute to the good of society. Jesus promised that those who develop themselves will be rewarded. By contrast, those who waste their talents will be held accountable (Matthew 25:14-30).

The income we receive through our efforts is entrusted to us by God, and it's our responsibility to use it properly. Common sense tells us that it is a good thing to earn as much as we are able—provided that we are earning our money honestly and responsibly. But at the same time, some people will choose willingly to give up the potential for higher income. Some feel a special calling from God to lead a simple life as they minister to others in a more intense way. And others turn down promotions (and pay raises) because new responsibilities require too much time away from their families.

Spending and Saving Money

So what should we do with the money we earn? This raises the issue of good stewardship.

God wants us to be honest and prudent in our dealings with money. Being honest involves never intentionally engaging in anything unethical or illegal. It means treating everyone with respect and never knowingly cheating or manipulating another person. Being prudent means being wise with our spending and rejecting the temptation to be careless, whimsical, or greedy. It also means establishing a budget and trying our best to minimize our debt.

Whether we are wealthy or poor, it's easy to become so attached to our belongings that we put our trust in them. When Jesus tells us to put our trust in God and to stop worrying about our material needs (Matthew 6:19, 24, 31), he is not telling us to be irresponsible. He is telling us to watch out, because money—and the way money can cause us to act—can separate us from God and from his love.

How we save and spend our money is a complex, individual issue. And yet our parameters as Christians are clear—be wise, be disciplined, be prudent. Yes, it is good to save our hard-earned money in order to buy a house or a car, or to pay for our children's education. Yes, we should put away money to meet our needs when we grow old. Investing is a good and prudent thing. But let us never allow our concerns about money to become like a god and overshadow our love for Jesus!

We are called to live simply. Simplicity means rejoicing in God's good creation and thanking him for every financial blessing. It means being grateful and content for all we have and being free from covetousness. Living simply means using money to build heavenly treasures, not earthly ones.

Giving

Finally, we are to give to those in need. This is perhaps the best way to build our heavenly treasures. In the Sermon on the Mount, Jesus tells us to build up heavenly treasures because our earthly treasures will eventually be worthless. We are simply stewards of our earthly treasures. Our money really belongs to God. There will come a day when our money will become utterly worthless. On that day, we will find out how much is in our heavenly bank accounts.

We all know how to give, and we all know how to keep for ourselves. On the one extreme, we can be like the widow who gave away all she owned (Mark 12:41-44). On the other extreme, we can be like the rich man who was indifferent to the needs of the poor beggar Lazarus (Luke 16:19-31). What is an appropriate balance for the majority of us?

If you are giving to your parish or are trying to be generous to your friends, try to give more. Ten percent is the biblical standard. If you cannot give 10 percent, make it your goal to increase your giving by 1 percent each year. Also, remember that giving should not be limited to finances. It can mean helping a neighbor, tutoring a child, visiting a nursing home, or even picking up trash alongside the road. St. Francis of Assisi taught that the more you give, the more you receive. God does bless those who give with a cheerful heart.

Building Heavenly Treasures

Earning and having money is not a sin. Yet if we allow ourselves to become too focused on money, it has the potential to dominate us, divide our marriages, and strain our relationship with Jesus.

Each of us needs to find out how to keep money in the proper perspective. Let's follow the words of Jesus to seek God first and to reject the notion that money can save us or make us happy. Love, not money, gives us peace, quiets our hearts, and unites our families. Jesus urged us to "strive first for the kingdom of God and his righteousness" (Matthew 6:33), and everything else we need will be given to us. Let us put our faith in God, not material security. As we lay our material goods at the foot of the cross, Jesus will transform them—using them to care for the poor and to build his kingdom. As we grow in trust that God will provide for us, we will also grow in generosity. How pleasing to God when he one day shows us the great treasures we have stored up in heaven!

CHAPTER 15

THE PROMISE OF RESURRECTION

Every Advent, the church offers us the vision of both the first and second coming of Christ, as her people cry out, "Amen! Come, Lord Jesus!" (Revelation 22:20). The prospect of the end of the world—or the end of our own lives—should fill believers with hope and expectation. We have been redeemed by Christ! Now we are looking forward to the day when Jesus comes to take us into his heavenly kingdom! Jesus himself told his disciples that even in the midst of the most tumultuous events, his followers should be able to "look up and raise your heads, because your redemption is drawing near" (Luke 21:28).

In this last chapter, let's take a look at the confidence and hope we can have as the truths we have talked about throughout this book make their way to our hearts. By taking the teachings of the church and the promises of Scripture personally, our fear of death will be broken. Neither will we fear the judgment to come, because we will trust that our lives are hidden with Christ in God (Colossians 3:3). In fact, we will look forward to—and even begin to long for—Jesus' second coming with joyful expectation.

A Living Hope

Informed by a doctor that he had only one month to live, St. Francis of Assisi—only forty-five years old but bedridden, almost completely blind, and in constant pain—replied lightheartedly: "And now, welcome Sister Death." He called two close brothers, Angelo and Leo, to his side and asked them to sing his beloved Canticle of Brother Sun. This time, however, he added a new stanza:

> All praise be yours, my Lord, through Sister Death,
> From whose embrace no mortal can escape.
> Woe to those who die in mortal sin!
> Happy those she finds doing your will!
> The second death can do no harm to them.
> Praise and bless my Lord, and give him thanks,
> And serve him with great humility.

Sure Promises

How could St. Francis be so joyful even in the face of suffering and death? We don't have to search far for the answer: Francis knew the love of his Savior. He was filled with an expectant hope that triumphed over any fear. This kind of hope—Christian hope—is not just a wish or desire that things will go well for us, whatever the odds may be. Rather, it is a firm expectancy based on the loving kindness of our Father in heaven. Through this divine gift of hope, we "place our trust in Christ's promises and rely not on our own strength, but on the help of the grace of the Holy Spirit" (*Catechism of the Catholic Church,* 1817).

With its emphasis on contracts and negotiations, society tends to think of promises as legally binding agreements that parties will act in a certain way—often with built-in caveats and loopholes. But for God, a promise is an unshakable pledge of love and blessing. His promises reveal his goodness and his desire to fill us with his life and love. There are no loopholes in this promise. There is no "fine print." Our lives are very secure when they are rooted in God's promise of eternal life.

The Promise of Eternal Life

God's desire that we be with him in heaven is one facet of the foundational promise he made at the very beginning of time. In his Letter to the Ephesians, St. Paul wrote that God "destined us in love to be his sons and daughters through Jesus Christ" (Ephesians 1:5). From the very start, God determined that he would invite us to be his children—people who knew his fatherly love and protection and who would take on his characteristics.

Nothing—not even sin or death—can triumph over God's purposes. Brothers and sisters, we are not alone in this world. We are members of God's family. And because we have a loving and generous Father, we can trust in Jesus' promise, "He who hears my word and believes him who sent me has eternal life; he does not come into judgment, but has passed from death to life" (John 5:24).

St. Peter wrote, "You are a chosen race, a royal priesthood, a holy nation, God's own people" (1 Peter 2:9). In his desire to bring us fully into his presence, God has bestowed a great dignity upon us. Do you know the hope of the resurrection? Do you know that God loves you and wants you to be with him forever? You don't have to earn his love. He was disposed to love you even before he created you. You can't make him love you any more than he does—which is completely—and nothing you do can make him stop loving you. He asks only that you turn away from sin and invite him into your life. Then the joyous prospect of eternal life with him will flow into your heart; the fear of death will fade away.

The Foundation of Our Hope

Our hope in the resurrection is firm not just because of God's promises but because it rests on the fact of Jesus' resurrection. Paul wrote, "If Christ has not been raised . . . your faith is in vain" (1 Corinthians 15:14). And we know that our faith is far from futile: "Christ has been raised from the dead, the first fruits of those who have fallen asleep" (15:20). Jesus is risen. He has conquered death. "Death no longer has dominion over him" (Romans 6:9)—nor over us. Now he invites all of us to be baptized into his life and live with him forever in heaven.

At one point in his ministry, Jesus told his disciples, "Fear not, little flock, for it is your Father's good pleasure to give you the kingdom" (Luke 12:32). He says that also to us today. Jesus wants us to be with him forever. He loves us and takes delight in us. It is natural to be concerned about our responsibilities and the welfare of our families. Indeed, we must. But God also wants us to be confident and joyful, trusting in his desire and his ability to bring us to heaven.

St. Francis knew that those who serve God and try to do his will have nothing to fear from death. Through baptism and faith in Jesus' death and resurrection, they are protected from the "second death" (see Revelation 21:6-8). Resurrection awaits us; the Holy Spirit is guarding it for us, even as he seeks to draw us closer to the Father in our daily lives. For all who have received the promised Spirit, death is the gateway to eternal life.

Raised with Christ

Throughout this book, we have seen how Jesus' resurrection life is not a promise that will be fulfilled only in some future existence. It is available to us *here and now,* even as we await its complete ful-fillment at the end of time. God doesn't make us wait for the final resurrection before we can experience life with him. It can begin even now as a foretaste of the glory that awaits us. In a sense, God has already "raised us up" with Christ (Ephesians 2:6).

What are some of the signs we can expect as a result of having been raised up with Jesus? We can experience God speaking to our hearts in prayer, assuring us of his love and giving us his strength. We can discover countless treasures in Scripture as the Holy Spirit fills our hearts with God's wisdom and consolation—his very thoughts. We can see long-standing patterns of sin fall away and find ourselves empowered to love other people beyond our human capabilities. All because the power of the resurrection is ours now!

We can experience this joy even in the midst of trials. St. Paul told the Philippian church, "Rejoice in the Lord always; again I will say, Rejoice" (Philippians 4:4). Why? "The Lord is at hand" (4:5). What's amazing is that he wrote these words while in prison, with the threat of execution hanging over him (1:19-26)!

Receive the Promise

Brothers and sisters, God wants to transform us. He wants to be very close to us and write his promises on our hearts and fill our minds with his truth. He wants to give us a "living hope" (1 Peter 1:3), not just an intellectual agreement to a set of doctrines. It is a hope we can experience as we learn the art and discipline of prayer, Scripture reading, and repentance. Without this living hope, we will remain bound by fear, especially the fear of death. No amount of reasoning or philosophizing will be able to break this fear. But when we allow Jesus to enter our hearts as a person, our lives will change. We will know we are safe in his arms. We will know that God will never forget his promises. We will know the Spirit's power to free us from sin and make us joyful witnesses to "the hope laid up for [us] in heaven" (Colossians 1:5).

Waiting in Joyful Hope

Through Christ, every promise of God that we have presented in this book is now available to us: freedom from sin, healing of wounded relationships, physical healing, joy, peace, and inner strength. Even if we find ourselves struggling against sin, our hope is secure if we have placed our lives in Jesus' hands. As St. Paul wrote: "He who did not spare his own Son but gave him up for us all, will he not also give us all things with him?" (Romans 8:32).

At every liturgy, we ask God to protect us and watch over us "as we wait in joyful hope for the coming of our Savior Jesus Christ." Brothers and sisters, God wants us to live every day in this "joyful hope" of tasting his presence and longing for the fullness that will be revealed when Jesus comes again.

Come to Me!

As we continue to deepen in our relationship with the Lord, not only will our fear of death fade—our fear of punishment will also begin to give way to an eager expectation of seeing Jesus face-to-face. We will begin to understand that he too longs for the day when he will be united with his bride, the church. That is why, as the church prays, "Come, Lord Jesus!" (Revelation 22:20), Jesus himself cries out, "Come to me, all who labor, . . . and I will give you rest" (Matthew 11:28).

Jesus knows how easily we can become immersed in the demands of day-to-day living and so lose sight of our heavenly inheritance. So every day he invites us, "Come to me." He knows how our "busyness" can overshadow the spiritual life he wants us to develop. Jesus frequently told his disciples to watch and wait as they eagerly prepared themselves for the day when they would stand before him and receive his kingdom.

No matter how hard we try, we will never know the day or the hour of Jesus' return—even Jesus said he didn't know (Matthew 24:36). In fact, the timing may not be as important to God as it seems to us. To him, a thousand years are as a day, and a day is as a thousand years (2 Peter 3:8). He is more concerned with the state of our hearts than with whether we know the details of the end times. Whether Jesus comes back tomorrow or in three hundred years, the primary question remains the same: "When the Son of man comes, will he find faith on earth?" (Luke 18:8). He will find faith if his people keep themselves prepared, ready to give an account for themselves before the Lord whose love burns away all sin (Romans 14:12).

Preparing for Christ's Return

Have you ever been to a foreign country where you felt totally lost? There might have been numerous signs telling you where to go, what to do, or what dangers to guard against—but all in a language you did not understand. If only you could have read the signs, you would have felt more secure! Similarly, we need to understand the language of the Holy Spirit so that we can read the signs of the times and know how to respond to God as he prepares us for the end (Matthew 24:32-33).

We are usually well aware of the physical realities around us—the seasons, the weather, our relationships, our health. What is true for our physical lives is equally true for our spiritual lives. Believers who are in touch with Jesus in prayer can be attuned to the "signs of the times" around them. As they grow in their understanding of how God is moving on the earth, they become more ready for Jesus' return. They can actually "hasten the day" by their prayer, obedience, and love (2 Peter 3:12).

When a lawyer asked Jesus to sum up the whole of the Jewish law, Jesus responded with two basic requirements: Love God wholeheartedly, and love your neighbor as yourself. Everything else, he said, flows from this (Matthew 22:36-40). That's how simple the gospel is! If we want to prepare for Jesus' return, our best course is to ask the Holy Spirit to empower us to obey these two fundamental commands. Let's look at two of Jesus' parables about the end times to see how important these commands are in God's eyes.

Loving God

The parable of the ten bridesmaids (Matthew 25:1-13) gives a pattern for loving God by allowing his presence to burn brightly within us. The difference between the "wise" and the "foolish" women was the amount of oil they provided for their lamps—oil that would feed the flame and surround them with light. How vital it is that we maintain God's presence in our hearts! By the Holy Spirit—the fire of God's love—we can see age-old patterns of sin and division fall away. Wounds from the past and fears for the future can be healed; we can know our Father's love more deeply. The "oil" we need is an attentive heart that hungers for more of the Holy Spirit.

It is true that the Holy Spirit is always present within us, but it is equally clear that there can be obstacles in our lives that limit our openness to the Spirit's power. Hence many believers pray for a greater outpouring of the Spirit. Just as the wise bridesmaids could not give oil to the foolish ones, we cannot expect other people to give us what only God can give—a greater thirst for God's life and a greater share in his Spirit.

Loving Others

The parable of the sheep and goats (Matthew 25:31-46) urges us to keep love for one another alive in our hearts. The generosity with which we reach out to others is a telling indicator of the degree to which we desire to see Jesus' kingdom established on earth. The point of the parable is not that feeding the hungry, providing clothing to the needy, or visiting the sick and the imprisoned piles up points for us in heaven. Rather, these acts of love are like a barometer, indicating how deeply we have been transformed by our relationship with God. The more we experience God's love in our prayer and worship, the more we will be moved to lay down our lives for others. The parable suggests that when Jesus comes as a judge, he will determine how much we love God by the way we have loved others.

These two great commands cannot be separated. When we meet another person, we are meeting someone Jesus loves—someone for whom he died. Whenever we love, feed, or give hope to others, the Spirit in us reaches out to share the good news of salvation with them. The best gift we can give anyone is to introduce him or her to the Father, Son, and Holy Spirit who can provide all that we need . . . and more. So we pray: "Lord, give us more of your Spirit. Empower us to love your people. Teach us how to bring your hope and your love to those who don't yet know you. Jesus, make us your disciples."

"Now Is the Day of Salvation"

Jesus' teaching on his second coming calls us to concentrate on today. We cannot relive yesterday. Tomorrow may never come. But today we can seek God wholeheartedly. Today we can live for Jesus. Today we can serve others. Today we can intercede for a powerful outpouring of the Holy Spirit to prepare the world for Jesus' return. So if we hear his voice, let us not harden our hearts (Hebrews 3:7-8). Instead, let us all take it personally and cry out, "Amen. Come, Lord Jesus!" (Revelation 22:20). And until he comes we can continue to sing St. Francis's song:

> Praise and bless my Lord, and give him thanks,
> And serve him with great humility.

RECEIVING FROM GOD . . . AND GIVING IT AWAY

What Is the Message of *The Word Among Us*?

St. Luke tells us that when the Holy Spirit came upon the apostles at Pentecost, a rushing wind from heaven filled the whole house where they were staying (Acts 2:2). In the midst of all the excitement, Peter addressed the crowd that had gathered outside in what was the first public preaching of Christ. Peter explained what was happening, but he also invited them to receive the Holy Spirit themselves. It's as if Peter knew instinctively that this gift of God was meant for everyone, and he was eager to give it away.

This rhythm of receiving God's gift and then giving it away runs throughout the New Testament and has been a hallmark of the church ever since. We see it in the lives of the saints, in the teachings of the church on evangelization, and in the witness of millions of everyday believers who step out of their comfort zones and share the love of Christ with those around them. In fact, it was out of this same desire to give away what God has given us that we began *The Word Among Us* magazine in 1981. So what is it that we first received and are now trying to give away? Actually, it's quite simple.

It was through the outpouring of grace in the Charismatic Renewal that the Holy Spirit revealed Jesus to us in a new and penetrating way. The revelation was so dramatic that it changed our lives. We felt as if God had awakened us to the possibility of an intimate, personal relationship with Christ—something many of us had originally thought was reserved only for the great saints. We were surprised, delighted, and not a little bit humbled that God would want us to know him so personally. And we were also convinced that this outpouring of grace and revelation was not just for us.

Over time, as our relationship with Jesus blossomed, we also began to learn what it meant to live in the Spirit. By pondering Scripture, studying the teachings of the church, and developing a prayer life, we discovered that our initial experience of Jesus—the beginning of a relationship with him—was meant to grow and deepen into an abiding, daily communion with the Lord (Romans 8:5). And this communion was meant to affect every aspect of our lives.

These two dimensions—growing closer to Jesus and living in the Spirit—became the central messages of *The Word Among Us* as well as the guiding themes in the development of this book.

A Personal Relationship

How can we even know that God wants his people to have a personal relationship with him? The best way to answer this question is to look at the Scriptures.

In its very first chapters, the Bible portrays human beings as having been created with a unique capacity for knowing God. Above all the other creatures on earth, only men and women are made in God's image and likeness. And the man, Adam, is described as a "living being" only after God himself breathes life into him (Genesis 1:26; 2:7). These images of intimacy and likeness to God tell us that God had something special in mind for the human race—something that sets us apart from the rest of creation.

Later, especially through the prophets, God made it clear that he wanted more for his people than sacrifice and obedience: He wanted a *relationship*. Through Jeremiah, he promised a new covenant in which he would write his law on our hearts, and in which every one of us can know him, "from the least . . . to the greatest" (Jeremiah 31:33-34). Through Ezekiel, he promised not just to give us a new spirit but to fill us with his own Holy Spirit (Ezekiel 36:26-27). And finally, through his greatest prophet, John the Baptist, he promised that Jesus would baptize—*fully immerse*—us in this Holy Spirit (Matthew 3:11; John 1:33).

At the Last Supper, Jesus went so far as to call us his "friends" and to tell us that we really could abide in his love in a deep and intimate way (John 15:4, 7-9, 10, 15). All of these passages—and so many more—point to God's deepest desire to pour his life and his love upon us all.

Beyond the Scriptures, we felt that the Spirit was leading us to some of the greatest saints in the church. People like John of the Cross, Bernard of Clairvaux, Ignatius of Loyola, Teresa of Avila, and Thomas Aquinas had a dramatic effect on our lives. Their life stories as well as their teachings resonated with our own experience and confirmed what we were learning again and again.

The Scriptures and the lives of the saints show us that God desires to know the people he created, but what does it mean for us ordinary men and women to experience a personal relationship with Jesus ourselves? It means encountering Jesus in an intimate way and experiencing a taste of his love, joy, and mercy in our lives. It means a growing desire to hear him speak to us through Scripture. It means seeing the Mass, confession, and all the sacraments of the church as personal, life-giving encounters with God. In short, it means experiencing an exchange of love with the God who has loved us from before time began.

Spiritual Transformation

As wonderful as it is, developing a living relationship with Jesus is only one part of what we sensed the Spirit was showing us. Equally important—and equally promising—is his desire to *transform* us. In fact, we can't have one without the other. We need to be in touch with Jesus if we want to be transformed. Likewise, any transformation from God means primarily growing closer to Jesus and becoming more like him.

Jesus once told his disciples: "Be perfect, therefore, as your heavenly Father is perfect" (Matthew 5:48). It may sound impossible, but Jesus wants us to know that he has given us everything we need to become perfect—that is, to become more and more like him. We don't have to wait until we die and get to heaven. Every day, we can be changed "from one degree of glory to another" (2 Corinthians 3:18).

St. Paul tells us that it is God's deep desire to "transform" us by the "renewal" of our minds (Romans 12:2). On the one hand, God is the only one who can show us the way to perfection. He is the only one who can transform us. On the other hand, we have an important part to play in this transformation process as well.

It's Up to Us . . . and God

We may never figure out exactly how much of our spiritual growth is our doing and how much is God's grace. But we do know that it is up to us to seek God's presence and to yield ourselves to him. It is up to us to learn, through prayer and daily examination, the ups and downs of our inner lives. Our part involves evaluating how we react to the good and bad events of our days. It involves asking how our emotions, memories, and imaginations affect the decisions we make. It involves determining which aspects of our lives we should treasure and develop, and which parts need to be put to death (Colossians 3:5).

But life in the Spirit is not just about our relationship with the Lord. It also has to do with the way the Spirit wants us to treat one another. That's why we devote so much space in *The Word Among Us* to reconciliation, healing wounded relationships, and marriage and family. It's also why we talk about broader social issues like the sanctity of human life, our duty to the poor, and the mission of the church in the world.

God has shown us that with the Holy Spirit's help, we really can take every thought captive and make it obedient to Jesus. He has convinced us that his own divine power is available to everyone to help demolish the arguments and pretensions that raise themselves against his will (2 Corinthians 10:5). We truly believe that it is possible for our minds to be renewed and for our lives to reflect the same kind of love that Jesus showed as he walked the earth. It may be a lifelong process, but it is possible. What's more, it is a joyful and exciting way to live!